Praise for *How to Sound Cultured*

'Damn. All my cheating secrets revealed. In book form.'

Stephen Fry

'Terrific. With almost miraculous concision, they combine biographical information and often quite bracing judgments with jokes, some great quotations and lots of arresting little facts.'

Daily Mail

HOW TO BE COOL

HOW TO BE COOL

THE 150 ESSENTIAL IDOLS, IDEALS AND OTHER COOL S***

THOMAS W. HODGKINSON

ICON

This edition published in the UK and USA in 2017
by Icon Books Ltd,
Omnibus Business Centre,
39–41 North Road, London N7 9DP
email: info@iconbooks.com
www.iconbooks.com

Previously published in the UK and USA in 2016 by Icon Books Ltd

Sold in the UK, Europe and Asia
by Faber & Faber Ltd, Bloomsbury House,
74–77 Great Russell Street,
London WC1B 3DA or their agents

Distributed in the UK, Europe and Asia
by Grantham Book Services,
Trent Road, Grantham NG31 7XQ

Distributed in the USA
by Publishers Group West,
1700 Fourth Street, Berkeley, CA 94710

Distributed in Canada
by Publishers Group Canada,
76 Stafford Street, Unit 300, Toronto, Ontario M6J 2S1

Distributed in Australia and New Zealand
by Allen & Unwin Pty Ltd,
PO Box 8500, 83 Alexander Street,
Crows Nest, NSW 2065

Distributed in South Africa
by Jonathan Ball, Office B4, The District,
41 Sir Lowry Road, Woodstock 7925

Distributed in India by Penguin Books India,
7th Floor, Infinity Tower – C, DLF Cyber City,
Gurgaon 122002, Haryana

ISBN: 978-178578-262-6

Typeset in Minion by Marie Doherty

Printed and bound in the UK by Clays Ltd, St Ives plc

Contents

CONTENTS

For my parents,
who are both extremely cool.

About the Author

About the author

Thomas W. Hodgkinson is the co-author of *How to Sound Cultured* (Icon, 2015) and author of the horror novel *Memoirs of a Stalker* (Silvertail, 2016). He writes a film page for *The Week*, travel articles for the *Daily Mail* and book reviews for *The Spectator*. A few years ago, he became the first person officially to swim from Albania to Corfu, where he spends a lot of his time.

Acknowledgements

Duncan Heath, Charlie Campbell, Andrew Furlow,
Anna Yermakova, Thomas Fink, Alastair Hall,
Hubert Van Den Bergh, Alice Long, Dominic Hodgkinson,
Nick Thompson, Alexandra Vishnevskaya, Hettie Harvey,
Crispin Ayshford Sanford, Matthew Slater, Tom Stevens,
Antalya Nall-Cain, Andrew Sentance, Philip O'Mahony,
Jack Churchill, Jonah Wyn Pugh, John Means Cooper,
John Lahr, Jocelyn Baines, Colin McKenzie,
Robert Hodgkinson, Annabel Long, Jeremy White,
Bertrand Pierret, Nicholas Allen, Martin Amis,
Gina Price, Theo Tait, Caroline Law, Jeremy O'Grady,
Miles Crawford, Jason Locke, Robert Posner, Mia Latter,
Daisy Aitkens, Mel Gibson, Benedict Cumberbatch,
Alexander Fiske Harrison, Mark Amory, Kitty Tait,
Anastasia Elisee, Marcus Scott-Barrett, Michael Bates,
Roseanne Kay, Jessica Mayberry, Tom Casdagli.

Cool: An Introduction

There's a story I remember being told by a friend when I was at school. Back in the 1970s, the actor Clint Eastwood – known for playing bestubbled, hard-bitten heroes – was being interviewed by the Irish chat show host Terry Wogan. 'So come on, Clint,' Wogan asked him chummily. 'How is it that you're so cool?' To which Eastwood responded by taking out a cigarette, flicking it up in the air, striking a match on the heel of his shoe, and then lighting the cigarette while catching it between his lips on its descent. After taking the first puff, he growled, 'I dunno, Terry. I guess it just happened that way.'

When I was told that story, I thought it was about the coolest thing I'd ever heard. So my first advice to anyone who wishes to know how to be cool is: take up smoking, learn a party trick, and maybe develop a trademark growl.

I'm kidding.

So what is my first advice?

These are deep waters. You don't want to plunge right in.

Before we go any further, there are four immediate questions raised by the very idea of a book bearing the brazen title of *How to Be Cool*, and they are these:

1) What is cool?
2) Where did it come from?

3) Has it changed?

4) Can it be taught?

With your permission, I'll give the brief, knee-jerk answers to these questions, and then offer my longer, more considered responses. The brief, knee-jerk answers are as follows.

'Cool' can't really be defined but it has something to do with style and something to do with emotional composure (aka 'keeping your cool'). It arose out of the New York jazz music scene and was taken up by Hollywood in the 1950s in movies featuring cool characters played by the likes of James Dean and Marlon Brando. The attitude became so popular with the young that the word 'cool' came to mean little more than 'good'. Yet in certain contexts it still retains something close to its earlier meaning. And this is something that cannot be taught. There are cool people and there are uncool people. You either have it or you don't.

Consider those claims, particularly the last one. Now I accept that there are certain physical attributes that can't be taught. You can't teach someone to be tall, for example, although it might be fun to try. But when it comes to character, almost anything can be taught. Virtue. Courage. And, yes, coolness too. So keep an open mind (an essential prerequisite of cool), read on, and see if you're persuaded.

1) What is cool?

I'm going to come right out and say it. I have identified the NINE DEFINING QUALITIES OF COOL.

These are the Nine Qualities that you need to know. You won't find them anywhere else. How did I come up with them? That will be revealed in due course. But for now, consider the Nine. How many have you got taped?

- Style
- Rebellion
- Recklessness
- Rootlessness
- Promiscuity/Celibacy
- Self-expression
- Flamboyance/Austerity
- Taciturnity/Eloquence
- Emotional self-control

We'd better unpack these a little. Style: You're physically coordinated and know how to dress. Rebellion: You question authority. Recklessness: You value present pleasure over future health. Rootlessness: You travel. A lot. Promiscuity/Celibacy: The point is that you're not into the whole monogamous commitment thing. Self-expression: You're somehow an artist. Flamboyance/Austerity: Either will do. Taciturnity/Eloquence: You make words count. Emotional self-control: You're pretty relaxed. You rarely lose it.

So how did I compile this list, these Nine Defining Qualities of Cool? I'm going to answer that. I am, but not straight away. We don't want to get bogged down in methodology.

2) **Where did it come from?**

Coolness isn't a 20th-century invention but it is a 20th-century phenomenon. That's to say, if you look back through the centuries, you can find examples of people who had some or most of the Nine Qualities. In the Middle Ages. In Ancient Greece and Rome. There were probably cavemen who were cool. In fact, now I come to think of it, there definitely were.

But it earned a name only in the 20th century when, for a perfect storm of reasons, an anti-establishment attitude began to exert an extraordinary mass influence among the young. This was an unprecedented cultural shift, which amounted to the rise of a new value system to rival those offered by morality or worldly success. We'd had rich. We'd had good. Now here was cool, which was something completely different.

The question of where cool came from is one that scholars have tried to answer literally, which is to say geographically. The art historian Robert Farris Thompson, for example, has a theory that its true origin was a quality called *itutu* (a blend of cool-headedness, playfulness and generosity) that was developed by the Yoruba and Ibo peoples of West Africa. It was carried to America in the 19th-century slave ships, where it hardened into a stance of silent but seething defiance.

Then, amid the burgeoning jazz music scene of 1930s New York, there was (we are told) a practice in some clubs of throwing open the windows in the early hours of the morning to let the cool air in, and blow away the smoke of a thousand cigarettes. As a result, the small-hours jazz playing style, which tended to be pretty laid-back, became known as 'cool jazz'. And later that 'coolness' somehow got linked to the rebellious attitude that was rooted in West African *itutu*.

None of this impresses me much. The meaning of a word isn't defined by origin but by usage. And in any case, where do they take us, these hypothetical theories that are at least partly based on anecdote? More interesting, I think, is to consider where cool came from in the sense of what caused it. What were the conditions, the catalysts?

This isn't, thank god, an academic study, providing rigorous proofs and scrupulous sources. A really thorough account of the rise of cool would need to be practically a roadmap to 20th-century culture. It would include every B-road, byway and lay-by. All we're aiming to do here is to find the right motorway and stick to it.

For the record, though, a comprehensive catalogue of the 'inciting incidents' (to use a screenwriting term) that combined to create cool would include not only the suppressed resentment of the cotton-picker (American slavery) and the relaxed intensity of musical improvisation (jazz and blues), but also the breezy confidence of the flapper (first-wave feminism) and the conservative prosperity of post-war America, which gave the young something to rebel against (juvenile delinquency). The historian Paul Fussell suggested that the horrors of the First World War had such a traumatic impact on the western psyche that, ever afterwards, the dominant cultural and philosophical mode became one of irony, which avoided emotion and rejected the old value systems. Coolness, to extend Fussell's thesis, was to the Second World

War what irony was to the First. Let's say that it was irony with style.

In an influential essay published in 1957, the celebrity novelist Norman Mailer argued that coolness was a philosophical position: a bleak existential reaction to the barbarity of the Holocaust on the one hand, and the fear of nuclear catastrophe on the other. With an unforgivable past and an unliveable future, there was nowhere left to exist but in the present. Mailer refers to this, rather startlingly, as the search for 'orgasm'. One of the dangers of writing about cool is that it's easy to get carried away. But, as often with Mailer, in the general cut and thrust of his theory, he may have had a point.

3) Has it changed?

The Austrian philosopher Ludwig Wittgenstein said, 'Whereof one cannot speak, thereof one must be silent.' But if that were taken seriously, there would be no such thing as journalism. In any case, I've always suspected that the old dog was just trying to get everyone to shut up, so that he could bang on uninterrupted. One may not, it's true, be able to speak with absolute authority about the meaning of the word cool, but that doesn't mean that what one says won't be worth saying. From its origins as a term to signify the opposite of warm (a cool breeze), the word has progressed and digressed through a bewildering range of meanings.

Here's a list, which I offer in roughly chronological order. We've had flapper cool, jazz cool, blues cool, Beatnik cool, Hollywood cool (aka juvenile delinquency cool), rock 'n' roll cool, hippy cool (aka counterculture cool), punk cool, yuppie cool, hip hop cool, grunge cool, hipster cool and geek cool.

There's a fear here of having left something out. It reminds me of the scene in *Blackadder the Third* when Dr Johnson proudly presents his newly finished Dictionary to the Prince Regent, declaring that it contains every word in the English language. In that case, says Blackadder, may I present my most enthusiastic 'contrafibularities'? Similarly, I brace wearily for the moment when someone mutters, 'I hope you've included "murk", or else exclaims in outrage, 'Don't tell me you've left out the stuntman Barry Gawithers?'

Inevitably, there will be omissions. No doubt there will be confusions too. There usually are, when it comes to cool. That's one of the cool things about it.

Cool refuses to be defined. It hates labels, even designer ones. And even cool people can sometimes get it wrong. The comedian Lenny Bruce liked to tell the story of the time he saw a guy with a beard in a coffee shop and went up to him and said, 'What's shaking, baby?' The man turned out to be a rabbi. And rabbis can't be cool, can they?

Not easily, no. In whatever era we're talking about, coolness defines itself in opposition to convention and authority. But here's the thing. If it succeeds – which is to say, if it catches on, as cool caught on in the 20th century – then it becomes more conventional, and therefore proportionately less cool. Several of my Nine Defining Qualities of Cool have been at least partly absorbed into the mainstream. I'm thinking particularly of rebellion, recklessness, promiscuity and self-expression.

Does this then mean that cool is dead? Does it mean that now, in order to be cool, you have to be uncool? I don't think so.

If you accept that cool defines itself in opposition to convention, then it will be around for as long as convention is around. And convention isn't going anywhere. Or at least, it isn't going far. The thing, you see, about convention is that it's conventional. (It just can't help itself.) It will always revert, sooner or later, to its natural position, which is to align itself with a value system that prioritises the security of health and home, the rewards of monogamous commitment, and the prospect of a steady job.

What this means is that there will always be a central core of cool, which defines itself against this central core of convention. I guess you could call it Classic Cool. It is this – this recurring idea of Classic Cool – that *How to Be Cool* is focused on.

4) Can it be taught?

The great myth of cool is that it's effortless. It's a masterstroke, this, like the Devil's success in persuading people that he doesn't exist. By persuading people that it's effortless, cool looks even cooler, while also ensuring that few will attempt to up their cool quotient and challenge it for position. Nevertheless a curious game of Grandmother's Footsteps still takes place, by which those wishing to become cooler will creep forward, ready to freeze at any moment, should Classic Cool suddenly whirl round and spot them trying.

But try they do and try they always have. Anyone

repeating the self-serving myth of effortless cool, I would first congratulate for understanding the First Rule of Coolness, which is to deny that there are any rules. Then I would point them in the direction of some of those who are widely regarded as the coolest of the cool. In almost every case, it's clear that they themselves learnt from cool role models, sometimes quite deliberately. Early in his career, Paul Newman was thought to be copying James Dean. James Dean was thought to have copied Marlon Brando. Muhammad Ali confessed that he had been inspired by the flair and flamboyance of the boxer Jack Johnson. David Bowie wrote songs acknowledging his admiration for Andy Warhol and Bob Dylan. As a young man, the aspirant author Hunter S. Thompson typed out the entirety of Ernest Hemingway's novel *A Farewell to Arms*. That's right. *He typed the whole thing out*, word for word, punctuation mark for punctuation mark, in the hope of learning what it felt like to write a cool masterpiece. There was nothing effortless about that.

So the First Rule of Coolness is to deny that there are any rules.

The Second Rule of Coolness is to choose your role models.

This is the method. We're not dealing, like some self-help books, in lessons and exercises. There is no homework. What *How to Be Cool* does is present a selection of possible role models (Idols) and relevant themes (Ideas and Ideals) for your consideration. And then you must make your choice, of the ones that speak to you particularly.

That about wraps things up. But I promised I would come clean about how I identified the Nine Defining Qualities. So here it is. I used an *a posteriori* method. By that I don't mean (tempting as it may be to suggest) that they came out of my posterior. What I mean is that instead of sitting back and deciding what I thought cool meant, and then picking my people and themes, I picked first and decided later. I picked the coolest people. I picked the coolest things. Then I considered what they seemed to reveal about the meaning of the word.

None of my Idols, incidentally, possesses all Nine Defining Qualities of Cool, though most would score pretty high on The Cool Test (which you'll find in the Appendix). There may be themes in this book that seem relevant to none of these qualities. I make no apology for that.

What I will do, though, is very briefly answer two more questions suggested by the title.

5) Is cool cool?

By this I mean: is cool a good thing? Is it desirable?

The answer to this is: yes and no. Or rather, yes and no and yes. Yes, because usage defines meaning, and cool is always used positively; it can't refer to a negative thing. No, because its Nine Defining Qualities may encourage a certain superficiality in outlook and self-destructiveness in style. But then finally yes, because many of those qualities do seem admirable even when viewed outside the prism of a cool value system: for example, the habit of questioning authority, the impulse to live creatively, and the knack of self-control.

6) Who is the coolest person ever?

There's a story told by the Greek historian Herodotus, in which the rich King Croesus asks the wise Solon, 'Who is the happiest of men?' He's hoping that Solon will reply, 'You, Croesus', since he was so stinking rich. But Solon (an Ancient Greek version of an anti-capitalist) wasn't having any of it. He starkly declared that the happiest of men was some guy Croesus had never heard of: an ordinary citizen named Tellus. Tellus, apparently, had lived to see all his grandchildren survive infancy. He then perished nobly in battle.

Personally, I'm with Solon up until the part about dying in battle. But he does make a good point, which is relevant to us here. The likeliest thing, of course, is that the coolest person who ever lived is someone we've never heard of.

All of which said, I did take the trouble to cast around and see if I could find anyone who possessed all Nine Defining Qualities of Cool. As I mentioned, none of my Idols gets full marks. Yet I did, nevertheless, identify one person who seems to have managed this remarkable feat: one who, if I'm honest, rather surprised me. It was Jesus Christ.

And with that I must leave you.

When I began writing, I threw a cigarette a long, long way up into the air. I have to stop writing now, in order to catch it in my mouth and light it.

Like so.

PART ONE:
IDOLS

This isn't a list of the 75 coolest people who ever lived. I think I probably need to repeat that, because admittedly, it's what it looks like: but this is *not* a list of the 75 coolest people in history. I could try to write that list, but it would be completely subjective, and tell you far more about me than anything else. If that's your wayward interest, Part Three caters to your whim.

No, what this is, or aims to be, is a list of the 75 people who have contributed most to defining or refining our idea of what 'cool' has come to mean. It should really be entitled 'Idols and Idolaters' since it includes 'cool-chasers' such as Quentin Tarantino and David Bailey, more notable for whom they perceive to be cool than for their own coolness (though neither does too badly). There's also the laboriously uncool Norman Mailer, included because he wrote an important essay on the topic. And one or two others whose reputation baffles, but who seem – who knows how? – to loom large in the imagination, once the mind starts skimming over the landscape of cool.

William Blake, poet and artist (1757–1827)

You've got to start somewhere. And if you take William Blake to be one of the fathers of the Romantic movement, and accept that the Romantic movement – which prioritised rebellious feeling over conventional common sense – was an important forerunner for the rise of cool, then the life and personality of William Blake seem as good a place to start as any. Add to that the fact that the poet Allen Ginsberg*, one of the founders of 1960s countercultural cool, idolised him, and is said to have enjoyed a series of ecstatic epiphanies while reading Blake's poetry and masturbating, then that settles it. We had better start with Blake.

The man was a visionary, and that's not meant loosely or lazily, but in the literal sense. He actually saw visions of angels and demons, whom he would paint in oils (the extraordinarily sinister sketch 'The Ghost of a Flea' is an example) and address in his verse. He was, after Michelangelo, the greatest poet-painter in history, and one of the few really important British visual artists. He was also widely believed to be barking mad, although the evidence for this largely consists of those diverting or disconcerting visions:

> Tiger, tiger, burning bright, In the forest of the
>   night …
> To see the world in a grain of sand, And a heaven
>   in a wild flower …

---

* If a name has an asterisk next to it, this means it has its own entry in the book and is therefore in the index.

2

Love seeketh only self to please, To bind another to
   its delight …

These sonorous phrases all flowed from Blake's pen, highlights
to poems of flickering brilliance, which, although little read
in his lifetime, with the benefit of hindsight can be seen to be
worth whole cantos of Byron's* bestsellers. Strangely enough,
the man's best-known lines today are the lyrics to the hymn
'Jerusalem' ('And did those feet in ancient time …'). What's
curious about it is that the mind behind these patriotic-
sounding sentiments was in fact passionately anti-monarchist.

Blake's unconventional views were one reason for his
obscurity in his lifetime, and also for the attraction he held
in the mid-20th century for the likes of Ginsberg, who wor-
shipped him not only for his rebelliousness, but also as a
prophet of free love. Blake's poem 'The Garden of Love' ima-
gines the ministers of organised religion 'binding with briars
my joys and desires'. Yet these apparently hippyish views were
not pursued in practice. A mainstay of the poet's life was his
wife Catherine, to whom he was faithful for 45 years.

Beau Brummell, dandy (1778–1840)

Lord Byron* once remarked that there were three great men
of his era: himself, Napoleon and Beau Brummell – but the
greatest of these was Brummell. What was his drift? Brummell
wrote no poetry worth reading. He led no armies into battle. He
is mainly credited with having popularised trousers. And ties.

And three-piece suits. But to be fair, this did constitute a complete rewriting of the rules of fashion. Before Brummell, men had worn elaborate wigs and flashy clothing. This, he declared, was absurd. On the contrary, the aim should be to dress as simply as possible but with scrupulous attention to detail. This has been the shimmering ideal of male fashion ever since.

Picture Oscars night. You can see all the women in their diaphanous or soigné outfits, with the plunging necklines and backlines, and the twills and the frills and the gimmicks. (There goes Björk* in her infamous 'swan dress'.) Yet the strange thing, if we weren't so used to it, is that the men are all dressed more or less identically in sleek black dinner jackets. That's Brummell's legacy. He was known as a 'dandy', which originally meant a man who dressed in a plain style, albeit one that was achieved by a vast concentration of effort. The story goes – although it presumably cannot have been true – that every day he spent five hours getting ready before venturing out of doors.

A dandy is also someone who elevates the art of dressing to a life philosophy. The implication is that your clothes aren't designed to decorate you. They *are* you. It doesn't matter if you're not from a posh or wealthy family. If you're the best-dressed man in the room, you're the best man in the room, and everyone else can go to hell. This may seem a little superficial, but it was actually revolutionary at a time when worth was more generally determined by breeding.

Brummell, who was from a middle-class background, earned the admiration of the dim, plump Prince of Wales with his daring style and insolent, insouciant manner. This is one of the man's main claims to being a forerunner to 20th-century cool: he was dispassionate, rude, and often very funny in his deliberately outrageous attitudes. When someone asked him if he really restricted his diet to meat and bread, or if he ever indulged in vegetables, he confessed, 'I once ate a pea.' Another time, a friend of his noticed that he had a limp. 'I hurt my leg,' Brummell explained sadly. 'The worst of it is, it was my favourite leg.' Eventually his inability to resist a sharp one-liner led to his downfall. The sulky Prince snubbed him at a party, and Brummell declared loudly to his neighbour, 'Who's your fat friend?' Denied royal patronage, he fell into debt and died in a French asylum, penniless and insane from syphilis. Nevertheless, if you are intent on ruining your life, publicly insulting the heir to the throne is a pretty cool way to do it.

Lord Byron, poet (1788–1824)

Forget the poetry and the prose. In Lord Byron's case, it was all about the pose. Club-footed; as handsome as hell; an aristocrat who disdained rank. A ladies' man with an interest in young boys. The darling of society, who shunned its invitations. A genius with a secret. A rake-hell. A hero. The important point wasn't really whether the young baron was all or some of these things, but that they were his reputation. For the 'Byronic' character type he pioneered, both in verse and in person, was hugely influential in the 19th century and became a template for cool in the 20th.

This didn't come about by accident. A lifelong

self-dramatist, Byron cultivated his image to such an extent that it's hard to tell in retrospect when his behaviour was the product of a bipolar personality and when it was deliberately put on with the aim of sealing his legend. After an artist once sculpted him, Byron complained, 'That is not at all like me. I look much more unhappy.' He used to sleep with his hair in curlers to preserve his mop of tousled locks. He also wrote endless B-movie-style narrative poems about Byronic heroes, often pirates*, who swagger around hinting at diabolical secrets in their past. Inevitably, his horde of readers speculated that he was writing about himself, which of course he was. Or rather, he was writing about himself as he wished to be perceived.

He married his wife, Annabella, for her money, and then treated her viciously. She issued divorce proceedings against him after a year, on the grounds of various sexual perversions, including an unproven but probable incestuous affair with his half-sister, Augusta. Byron fled England, never to return. This rather suited him. He was, if anything, even more popular on the continent. He wrote horror stories with Shelley on Lake Geneva, had a ball in Venice with a series of Italian hotties, and finally, in a wild attempt to invest his dissolute life with purpose, sailed to Greece to fight against the Turks in the cause of freedom. In the event, he caught a fever and died at the age of 36.

Sarah Bernhardt, actress (1844–1923)

The playwright Oscar Wilde once asked the actress Sarah Bernhardt, 'Do you mind if I smoke?' 'I don't mind if you burn,' she replied. Although it's probably too good to be true, this serrated riposte captures the essence of Bernhardt's devil-may-care reputation. She wasn't particularly beautiful, but enjoyed a string of affairs with everyone from the novelist Victor Hugo to the Prince of Wales. As an actress, she had a rather hammy style and a weak, breathy voice. Yet through sheer charisma she earned the reputation of being the greatest actress of her era. Or as the novelist Mark Twain put it, there are 'good actresses, great actresses, and then there is Sarah Bernhardt'.

Henry James may have been closer to the mark when he described her as a genius at self-promotion. Her first publicity coup came in 1862 when, as a young actress struggling to make her name on the Parisian stage, she called the leading lady a 'miserable bitch' and slapped her face. By the end of the week, she was out of a job, but everyone knew who she was. A lifelong fabulist, the Divine Sarah, as many called her, sustained her celebrity by telling outlandish stories about herself and behaving with ostentatious eccentricity. She liked to sport a hat adorned with a stuffed bat, and kept a tame alligator she called Ali-Gaga. She also developed an odd habit of sleeping in coffins, explaining that it helped her to get to grips with her more morbid tragic roles. Her choice of those roles also seems self-conscious. Her decision to play Hamlet*, for instance (one of the most challenging male characters in the theatrical repertoire), was itself a feminist statement, while her penchant for biblical parts was deliberately designed to shock.

Her legacy rests as much on her personal style – in

particular, the display she made of not giving a damn – as it does on her dubious thespian skills. While touring in England, she made no effort to disguise the illegitimacy of her son at social events. On the contrary, she asked that on entering a room the two of them should be announced as 'Mlle Bernhardt, and her son'. That got the point across. To any questioning or criticism of her behaviour, the Divine Sarah tended to reply with a Gallic shrug and the phrase 'Quand même'. This loosely translates as, 'Do I look like I care?'

Arthur Rimbaud, poet (1854–91)

He was Bob Dylan's* favourite poet. Henry Miller was a fan. The three principal Beatniks*, Jack Kerouac*, William Burroughs* and Allen Ginsberg*, were all crazy about him. So what was it about the decadent French poet Arthur Rimbaud that got them pumped? After all, he was clearly a total bastard. What else can you conclude about someone who, on one occasion, defecated on a café table because he was bored, and on another, added sulphuric acid to someone's drink as a joke?

One reason why he has met with such passionate admiration is that he managed to write brilliant poetry while off his head on opium, absinthe and other stimulants. The implication is that he may have written so well *because* he was off his head, which therefore provides a useful pretext for other writers to get off their heads, too. It has to be admitted that Rimbaud himself believed there was a causal link between intoxication and inspiration. In a letter he wrote to a friend when he was seventeen, he declared that the poet who wishes to become a visionary must do so by what he called the 'long, immense et raisonné dérèglement de tous les sens': which is to say, a 'vast, sustained and deliberate disruption of all the senses'. Rimbaud believed that, in the case of the great Ancient Greek poets, verse had arisen directly from the soul, whereas the writers of his day, by contrast, were merely playing pompous artificial literary games. The best way to prise oneself free of these disgraceful conventions, Rimbaud argued, was by getting wrecked, and that is what he did.

Running away from his tediously provincial home at sixteen, he threw himself into a life of artistic decadence, which centred on a violent homosexual relationship with the poet Paul Verlaine, who eventually tried to kill him but only succeeded in shooting him in the wrist. None of this would be of much interest if Rimbaud had written bad poetry. To his fans, his easy early stuff (e.g. *Le Dormeur du val*, in which someone you think is asleep turns out to be dead) and his later, harder style (for instance, the autobiographical prose poem *Une Saison en enfer*) are both in their different ways indispensable. Having said all he had to say, Rimbaud put down his pen at the age of twenty and literally never wrote another poem. Instead he travelled to Abyssinia, where he worked as a coffee merchant and gun runner. This is one of the things that most astonishes about Rimbaud: that he packed two such different lives into such a short span. He died of bone cancer at the age of 37.

Isadora Duncan, dancer (1877–1927)

The sculptor Auguste Rodin described her as 'the greatest woman the world has ever known'. The choreographer George Balanchine was less impressed. He remembered 'a drunk fat woman ... rolling around like a pig'. Doubtless the two men saw the American dancer Isadora Duncan at different stages in her career, since in later life she lost the lithe figure she'd honed as a girl growing up in California, and became rather rotund. A compulsive rebel, she rejected the present (describing the ballet of her day as 'sterile gymnastics') in favour of the past – specifically the ideals associated with the culture of Ancient Greece. Here, she was convinced, would be found the essence of dance, in its origins as a sacred act. She spent long hours in the British Museum in London, scrutinising the dancers depicted on Ancient Greek vases. Combining inspiration from this and other sources (for instance, the motion of the sea), she developed her system of 'natural movement', which would form the bedrock of modern dance.

Freedom was her watchword. Freedom of movement: she performed barefoot and in flowing Hellenic-style clothes, which afforded appreciative fans the sight of her bare legs and an occasional flash of bosom. Freedom of political expression: on stage in Boston, she declared her sympathy with Communism by baring one breast and waving a red scarf, shouting, 'This is red and so am I!' And freedom of sexuality: she produced two children out of wedlock, and had affairs with both men and women, including the alcoholic Russian poet Sergei Esenin, and the poet and playwright Mercedes de Acosta (who would later enjoy a relationship with Greta Garbo*).

All of which is a roundabout way of saying that Duncan was one of the original hippies. In a macabre twist, however, her devotion to freedom led to her death in grotesque circumstances. In 1927, in Nice, she climbed into a car with a young car mechanic she fancied, threw a long and flowing scarf over her shoulder, and declared, 'Adieu, mes amis! Je vais à la gloire!' (Goodbye, my friends! I go to glory!) It's a terrific parting shot for almost any situation, but it doesn't make much sense in this case. More likely, as some have reported, what she actually said was, 'Je vais à l'amour!', referring to the way she hoped her evening would pan out. As the car raced along, her flapping scarf caught in one of its wheels. Duncan was flung out onto the road like a rag-doll, her neck broken and, it's said, almost severed.

Coco Chanel, fashion designer (1883–1971)

'I may be French, but my pussy is international,' Coco Chanel once declared, rather startlingly. She might have made a similar claim about her impact on fashion, which is hard to exaggerate. For centuries, women had been constrained not only by restrictions in rights and education, but also by the clothes they were obliged to wear, which literally made it hard to move. The personally liberated Chanel freed her sex by creating designs that were both chic and practical: stripy sailor tops, espadrille shoes, bell-bottom trousers, and perhaps most famously, the 'little black dress'. Male fashion journalists were horrified by the 'garçonne' (tomboy) styles of the Chanel line. 'No more bosom, no more stomach, no more rump,' one lamented.

Chanel broke taboos in her personal life too. From a poor working-class background, she rose to be one of the richest women in France. She never married, but had a string of affairs, some of which lasted for years. Asked why she had never tied the knot with the staggeringly wealthy Duke of Westminster despite their decade-long relationship, she replied, 'There have been several Duchesses of Westminster. There is only one Chanel.' She did, however, acquire a couple of unfortunate attitudes from His Grace, including his violent homophobia and anti-Semitism. A cloud has been cast over Chanel's memory by the discovery that she seems to have collaborated with the Nazis during the Second World War. It wouldn't have been in her character to admit fault or apologise for it. 'The most courageous act,' she once observed, 'is still to think for yourself.'

Lead Belly, singer (1888–1949)

'Bad Nigger Makes Good Minstrel.' Thus ran the headline on an article in *Life* magazine in 1937: a three-page spread about an extraordinary blues singer and convicted murderer named Huddie Ledbetter, more commonly known as Lead Belly. The piece was accompanied by a photograph of him playing guitar, with the caption, 'These hands killed a man.'

Back in 1918, he had shot dead his cousin's husband during a row over a woman. After seven years in jail, he secured his release by writing a song for the Texas governor, begging for clemency.

A strong man with a violent temper, Lead Belly was again locked up in 1930, this time for attempted homicide. Salvation came in the form of John and Alan Lomax, a father and son team of musicologists travelling the American south recording authentic folk and blues songs. After hearing Lead Belly perform in prison, they successfully lobbied for his release. This granted, he joined John on the road, working as his driver, and in the process expanding his already considerable musical repertoire. (He was said to have the ability to hear a song once, then perform it note-perfectly.) The Lomaxes have been accused of exploiting Lead Belly by, for example, encouraging him to perform in prison clothes, to play up to his bad-boy image. Yet he also benefited from the association. Thanks to them, many traditional songs were recorded for the first time ever by Lead Belly, including 'Goodnight Irene' and 'Where Did You Sleep Last Night?'

The latter number was covered by Nirvana on their MTV *Unplugged* album, with a preamble in which Kurt Cobain* describes Lead Belly as his 'favourite performer'. Part of the reason was that he was a great, soulful blues singer who displayed enormous skill in mastering the cumbersome twelve-string guitar. (The feat has been notably managed by only a few other guitarists, including Led Zeppelin's Jimmy Page.) Evidently, though, it was also that he could claim possession of the holy grail of music: authenticity. When Lead Belly sang of picking cotton, working in a chain gang, or being imprisoned for murder, he didn't only seem to know what he was singing about.

Dorothy Parker, journalist, poet and wit (1893–1967)

There's a garden in Baltimore, outside the headquarters of the National Association for the Advancement of Colored People. And in that garden is a plaque, whose inscription reads: 'Here lie the ashes of Dorothy Parker (1893–1967) … For her epitaph she suggested, "Excuse my dust."'

There were two sides to Parker, light and dark, which operated simultaneously. Broadly speaking, the first half of her life was devoted to being arguably the first successful female epigrammatist in history: sassy, liberated, the original fast-talking, fast-living New York chick. Her humour was wry, acerbic, morbidly preoccupied with suicide (an act she dismissed because there is no attractive, convenient way of managing it) and often very funny, never more so than when her verbal barbs were directed at herself. Her accolades were substantial – she won awards for her short stories and two Oscar nominations for her screenplays – but she always presented herself as a gloomy under-achiever. She claimed, for instance, to be 'the toast of two continents, Greenland and Australia'. Whenever the telephone rang, she used to murmur, 'What fresh hell is this?'

That joke contained a dark grain of honesty. Parker was

an alcoholic, for whom happiness proved elusive. After her first marriage failed, she embarked on a string of affairs, one of which, with a well-known writer, resulted in a pregnancy that she aborted. (Characteristically, she cast a veil of humour over the episode, observing, 'How like me to put all my eggs in one bastard.') If her private life was chaotic, she made up for it in later life, increasingly devoting herself to altruistic causes. She set up the Hollywood Anti-Nazi League at a time when the movie industry's relations with Hitler's murderous regime were uncomfortably cosy, and she marched in the civil rights campaign with Martin Luther King. It was to King that, in her will, she left all her worldly goods.

Amelia Earhart, aviator (1897–1937)

On the afternoon of 20 May 1934, a slender, bob-haired pilot landed her Lockheed Vega monoplane in a field in Ireland. A bewildered farmhand asked her, 'Have you flown far?' 'From America,' the woman replied. For this was the aviation pioneer Amelia Earhart, who had just completed the first transatlantic flight by a woman. Apart from the adrenaline kick of flying, her life was devoted to the belief that pretty much anything a man could do, a woman could do too, and to becoming the visible embodiment of that principle.

As a girl growing up in Chicago, she collected newspaper cuttings about successful women. Later, after catching the flying bug, she cut her hair short in the manner of other female aviators. The style suited her, with her large eyes and pronounced cheekbones, although it was controversial at the time. She is said to have had an affair with the father of the author Gore Vidal, who didn't propose as he 'didn't want to marry a boy'. Instead Earhart married the publisher George Putnam, but on her own terms. She kept her name, and handed him a letter on their wedding day informing him that she didn't expect either of them to observe a 'medieval code of faithfulness'.

What sealed Earhart's fame was dying young in circumstances that have become shrouded in mystery. In 1937 she set off with navigator Fred Noonan to circumnavigate the globe. After completing 22,000 miles, they failed to find Howland Island, a tiny landing strip in the middle of the Pacific Ocean, and were never heard of again. Outlandish conspiracy theories* arose as to what had happened to them. Some believed they'd been captured and executed by the Japanese; others that Earhart had been on a secret mission for the US government, which required her to disappear deliberately, so a Navy rescue operation could be launched that would offer an excuse to photograph all the Pacific islands in preparation for the Second World War. Most likely, Earhart and Noonan simply missed their stopping point and plunged into the sea.

Humphrey Bogart, actor (1899–1957)

The guy was short. Let's say around 5ft 8in. He was also bald. His wig-maker Verita, who doubled as his mistress, accompanied him everywhere, carrying a suitcase containing ten hairpieces, with names ranging from 'cocktail' to 'shaggy'. He even came from a privileged background, starting out playing preppy characters on stage in New York. He is said to have been the first to deliver the line 'Anyone for tennis?' Yet the actor Humphrey Bogart eventually became synonymous with a character type that is the very essence of cool: bruised, cynical, but ultimately heroic.

Bogart – or 'Bogie', as he was known – rose to prominence playing gangsters*, snarling villains who get shot in the final reel. It wasn't until 1941's *The Maltese Falcon* that he progressed to the noble type. By then, his props and tics were established: the mac and fedora hat, the occasional leer or sneer, and his characteristically slurred speech. As with Marlon Brando*, Bogie's distinctive lisp – he spoke like a ventriloquist, barely moving his mouth – came about by chance. He had a scar on his upper lip, caused by a childhood accident. As a result, he always sounded like he'd had a couple of drinks. Which quite often, he had. Bogie was a determined drinker, his preferred poison being whisky and soda, which he referred to as 'loudmouth' because it tended to loosen his tongue (if not his lips). Occasionally it stood him in good stead. While filming *The African Queen* in the Belgian Congo in 1950, the crew all came down with dysentery, apart from Bogie and the director John Huston, both of whom had been surviving entirely on canned food and booze. 'Whenever a fly bit Huston or me, it dropped dead,' he later recalled.

Bogie wasn't the greatest actor who ever lived, but he was one of the greatest movie stars. It was the weary, almost-beaten-but-not-quite quality he brought to every role, with his sardonic mouth and gentle eyes, that mulish stubbornness that warned you not to try any funny business. He liked to be pugnacious in his private life, too. On meeting the novelist John Steinbeck, he immediately declared, 'Hemingway* says you're a bad writer.' His opening gambit to Frank Sinatra was equally punchy. 'They tell me you have a voice that makes girls faint. Make me faint.'

Marlene Dietrich, actress and singer (1901–92)

JFK and his father. Gary Cooper. Greta Garbo*. Josef von Sternberg. Maurice Chevalier. Frank Sinatra. David Niven. Jean Gabin (for several years). Douglas Fairbanks Jr. Marilyn Monroe. John Wayne. George Bernard Shaw. Kirk Douglas. Edith Piaf. Yul Brynner (for a decade). Erich Maria Remarque. Jimmy Stewart. What do these luminaries have in common? The answer is that they all, including the women, are believed at one time or another to have had an affair with the imperious screen siren and singer of sultry or sentimental songs, Marlene Dietrich.

She first came to fame in such films as *The Blue Angel* and *Morocco*, both directed by her lover Sternberg and released in 1930. In the first, she sang her torch song 'Falling in Love Again' (which doesn't have a lot to do with love). In the latter, she appears as a nightclub singer in top hat and tails, who kisses a startled female guest full on the mouth. These were to become the keynotes of the Dietrich persona: the Teutonic, cigarette-smoke-swathed femme fatale, haughtily bisexual and wryly obsessed with sex, but only if it was available on her own terms. Whatever else you might want to say about her (and there are a few things that spring to mind), she was no softie. When her thirteen-year-old daughter from an early marriage came to her in tears, lamenting that she had been sexually abused by a female nanny, Dietrich snapped, 'You're not dead. Deal with it.'

When the Nazis tried to bribe her to return to her native Germany and become their poster girl, she bluntly refused. (She later hatched a scheme to murder Hitler using a poisoned hairpin, but was talked out of it.) During the war she performed tirelessly for the US troops within firing range of the enemy. Asked why she risked her life in this way, she replied, 'Decency.' Despite being a limited actress and singer, with an accent she never lost and an endearing lisp of her Rs ('Dietwich'), she was a consummate, chameleonic performer. In the western *Destry Rides Again* (1939) she revealed a talent for broad comedy. She extended her career beyond its expected shelf life with a gruelling cabaret tour until ill health brought on by age and alcoholism made this impossible.

She then retired to her Parisian apartment, where she lay low for the rest of her life, in order to preserve her mystique. When a paparazzo climbed to her window in the hope of snatching a picture of her in her decline, the outraged star shot at him with a starting pistol.

Anaïs Nin, author (1903–77)

Anaïs Nin was a failure for most of her adult life. Publishers gave her a wide berth and she was reduced to self-publishing. Then, aged 63, she published the heavyweight diaries she had been scribbling at since she was eleven, and they were hailed as a masterpiece. In the permissive 1960s, the critics were bowled over not only by her frankness about sex and piquant anecdotes involving some of her better-known friends and lovers (who included Henry Miller, Antonin Artaud, John Steinbeck and Lawrence Durrell), but also by the lyrical, impassioned eloquence of her prose.

After her death, there was a backlash. It emerged that she had been married to two men at the same time, apparently without either of them knowing. A collection of erotic stories she had written, *Delta of Venus*, was published for the first time, with the consequence that some dismissed her as a second-rate pornographer. She had written the work on commission for a private collector, rather than in a spirit of high literary seriousness, yet the book is better and more important than that makes it sound. The first story, 'The Hungarian Adventurer', for example, starts out like standard male wish-fulfilment. Its protagonist, known as the Baron, is basically irresistible to women. But it gradually emerges as a disturbing cautionary tale. The Baron ends up depraved, abusing his own children (first his daughters and finally his son) in his agonised hunger for satisfaction.

Nin's achievement stands, bloody but unbowed. She was one of the first to write, and write well, about sex from a woman's perspective, a pioneer, in other words, whose indebted descendants include the *Fifty Shades of Grey* author E.L. James. And she demonstrated by her example how it was possible for a woman to survive, and thrive, in a male-dominated literary world, not least by being at least as sex-obsessed and self-obsessed as most of her lusty and egotistical male rivals. Among other things, she is remembered for remarking, 'We do not see things as they are, we see them as we are.' It was an observation that was particularly true in her own case.

Greta Garbo, actress (1905–90)

Strange to say, but it isn't easy to be beautiful *and* sexy. Sexy women don't tend to be beautiful, and beautiful women aren't sexy as often as you might think. Yet one who managed both was Greta Garbo, of whom the critic Kenneth Tynan remarked that what he saw in other women drunk, he saw in her sober. The Swedish actress rose to fame in silent movies, in which her Scandinavian accent was no handicap. Her studio MGM was terrified that the advent of sound to cinema would put paid to her career. They decided to take the gamble and go for it. What choice did they have?

'Garbo talks!' the publicity poster screamed, advertising her first talkie, 1930's *Anna Christie*. In the event, the film was a smash hit. The MGM suits later tried a similar tagline after casting the star, who had previously been known for playing gloomy femmes fatales, in her first comedy. 'Garbo laughs!' the poster bellowed. And audiences laughed too. The film, 1939's *Ninotchka*, in which she deadpans hilariously as a mirthless Russian tourist in Paris, was another Garbo classic.

The actress retired soon afterwards at the age of just 36, and thenceforth avoided the limelight. As a consequence, she became notorious as a recluse, forever associated with the phrase (which wags always deliver through a thick Swedish accent), 'I want to be alone.' Yet her reclusiveness has been exaggerated. As she herself put it, she only ever said she wanted to be *left* alone. She was no Howard Hughes or J.D. Salinger*. However, she does seem to have been a morose type, who tenaciously guarded her privacy. Her co-star and lover John Gilbert repeatedly proposed to her and she sometimes accepted but always backed out as the date drew near. 'I was afraid he would tell me what to do and boss me,' she explained. 'I always wanted to be the boss.'

As an actress, she was difficult to work with, insisting that screens were set up so random crew members couldn't watch her work. 'If I am by myself,' she said, 'my face will do things I cannot do with it otherwise.' Her performances in movies such as *Grand Hotel* (1932) and *Queen Christina* (1933) support the claim. She was a superb film actress, among the first to master the discipline of acting for the camera. As the director Clarence Brown put it, 'Garbo has something behind the eyes that you couldn't see until you photographed it in close-up. You could see thought.'

Josephine Baker, dancer (1906–75)

Josephine Baker was the first black woman in history to be an internationally renowned entertainer. Born in Missouri, and married twice in her teens, she started out performing in New York as the last dancer in a chorus line: a role that, according to music hall tradition, required her to dance badly on purpose, hamming it up for laughs, only to reveal her true skill at the end when she would perform a breathtaking solo dance. From Hamlet* to Humphrey Bogart* in *Casablanca*, this trope of the no-hoper who turns out to be the hero would be a key narrative pattern in the history of cool.

In Baker's case, it was played out on the larger scale, too. After she moved to Paris in the 1920s she became a star, best-known for her so-called *Danse sauvage* in which she performed in little more than a skirt made of artificial bananas. In the process, she played up to white perceptions of black culture, yet subverted them too by sending up the stereotype. A clown who was also a sex symbol, she later reinvented herself as a heroine of the Resistance and Civil Rights movement.

Thanks to her fame, Baker was permitted more freedom of travel than most during the Second World War. She used to transport information important to the Resistance either written in invisible ink on her music scores, or else concealed in her underwear (trusting that, as a celebrity, she was unlikely to be strip-searched). Her most famous song was '*J'ai deux amours*', in which she named America and Paris as her two great passions. Paris reciprocated, but America wasn't so sure. Baker stirred up resentment in the US by refusing to perform to segregated audiences. Then, in the 1950s she marched on Washington with Martin Luther King, and after he was assassinated, an idea was even mooted that she should take over as leader of the movement.

Lee Miller, photographer (1907–77)

When they make the film of the life of the fashion model, muse, Surrealist, and war photographer Lee Miller, they won't need to exaggerate. Her career started when she was almost run over by a car in the deafening streets of Manhattan. The man who pulled her to safety in the nick of time turned out to be Condé Nast, the publisher of *Vogue*. Struck by Miller's sleek androgynous beauty, he put her on the cover of his magazine. But it wasn't enough for her to be a pretty face. She envied the talent that she saw on the other side of the camera, too. Resolving to learn from the best photographer in the world, she moved to Paris, and sought out Man Ray.

Ray told her he didn't take students, but she insisted and soon became his lover. He later learnt, rather to his dismay, that she didn't think this entailed that she should be faithful to him. Male artists tend to believe that they have a licence to sleep around, but they're not thrilled if female artists do the same. Miller, it turned out, *was* an artist: a gifted photographer who took some of the Surrealist images that were credited to Ray. She also produced a wonderful series of portrait photographs of her friends, who happened to be among the most famous artists and writers of the time, including Pablo Picasso, Jean Cocteau, Paul Éluard, Max Ernst, Henry Moore and Oskar Kokoschka.

Later she added war photographer to her CV. She was with the US troops, on commission for *Vogue*, when they entered the Buchenwald and Dachau concentration camps. The mud from the camps was still on her boots when she visited Hitler's apartment in Munich. She decided to take a bath and the photograph of the nude Miller in the Führer's tub (snapped by her colleague David E. Scherman) has become iconic: an emblem of the triumph of liberal values over Fascist oppression.

In later life she became an alcoholic, tormented by the memory of her wartime experiences. Living in Sussex with her husband, the artist and writer Roland Penrose (who was eventually knighted, meaning she became Lady Penrose), she amused herself by concocting Surrealist-style recipes in the kitchen, which included blue spaghetti and cauliflowers shaped to resemble breasts.

Martha Gellhorn, journalist (1908–98)

The writer Martha Gellhorn often remarked, rather irritably, that she didn't want to be remembered only as a footnote in the life of the novelist Ernest Hemingway*, to whom she was married from 1940 to 1945. She avoided that fate, just about. Born in St Louis, Missouri, she was brought up by her suffragist mother to believe there was nothing a man could do that a woman couldn't do too, if she put her mind to it. Determined to be the living proof of this general rule, she became a hard-drinking, hard-living novelist, travel writer and war correspondent.

This last string to her bow came about after she met Hemingway in 1936 and hatched a plan that they would both travel to Spain and write about the Civil War. The shared experience led to a romance and ultimately marriage. However, Gellhorn found she disliked being married to a man who was her superior as a novelist, while for his part he didn't relish the widely held perception that she was the better war correspondent. Marital bliss degenerated into resentment and recrimination. The final straw came in 1945 when he agreed to cover the Allied invasion for *Collier's* magazine, which had traditionally employed Gellhorn. Nevertheless, she contrived to land in Normandy on D-Day, the only woman to do so. She was also among the first journalists to report from Dachau concentration camp.

As a reporter, Gellhorn excelled at conveying the private impact of public events. 'War happens to people, one by one,' she once declared. 'That is really all I have to say.' She went on to cover the Vietnam war and the Arab-Israeli conflict. In her private life she displayed a hard streak, verging on the cruel. After divorcing Hemingway, she never remarried. Being single, she said, was 'neater'. She adopted an Italian son, whom she later hounded about his perceived ingratitude, drug habits and weight, stipulating in her will that his inheritance depended on his not being obese. One thing none could doubt was Gellhorn's courage, a quality that characterised both her life and the leaving of it. She killed herself by rational suicide at the age of 89, on learning that she had terminal cancer.

Robert Johnson, musician (1911–38)

The story goes that Robert Johnson once met the Devil at a crossroads in rural Mississippi. The latter took his guitar, tuned it for him, played a couple of songs, and then handed it back. From that moment forth, Johnson, who had previously been a mediocre guitarist, displayed a diabolical skill. And what, according to those who believed this tale, did Johnson give the Devil in return? His soul, of course. As he travelled from place to place, he would impress the ladies with his musical skills, charming them into bed if he could. But he paid the price when a jealous husband spiked his whisky with poison. Some say Johnson ended his life in agony, crouched on all fours and howling like a dog.

The legend of this Faustian pact is a kind of creation myth for the blues itself. Partly as a result, Johnson is often referred to as 'the father of the blues'. But the truth is that there were blues players before him and ones who were more influential, at least at the time. Johnson recorded just 29 songs, none of which was a huge hit at first. It was only after they were reissued in 1961 that his talent was recognised, particularly by British musicians. The Rolling Stones guitarist Keith Richards* says he was blown away by the musical virtuosity when he heard Johnson tracks such as 'Hellhound on my Trail'. The guitar playing was so sophisticated he was convinced that two people must be playing the instrument. Eric Clapton was equally impressed by Johnson's soulful, rather high-pitched singing, which he once described as 'the most powerful cry you can find in the human voice'.

Behind the dark legend and shining reputation, Johnson himself remains obscure. The best-known photograph we have of him shows a slender, mischievous-looking figure, nattily dressed in a pinstripe suit. His long fingers, gripping the strings of his guitar, resemble claws. The sides of his hat's brim lend his silhouette the suggestion of two pointy ears. The infernal myth, in other words, continues to colour our perception. One thing we can say for certain: if the person Robert Johnson met at the crossroads really was the anti-Christ, then it's true what they say about the Devil having all the best tunes.

Tennessee Williams, playwright (1911–83)

Are actors cool? Don't they do little more than recite lines that have been written for them, and behave as they're instructed by the director? In the case of film actors, they're often required to say the same lines over and over again, like naughty schoolboys, until they get it right. Is that cool? Whatever your answer, spare a thought for whoever creates these heroic or anti-heroic characters according to his or her own value system. Spare a thought, that is, for Tennessee Williams.

An alcoholic homosexual from Mississippi, with a slick lick of hair and a dodgy 'tache, Williams wrote some of the greatest American plays of the 20th century, which were later adapted into some of the greatest movies. He had the good fortune to coincide with the rise of cool, so he got Marlon Brando* playing his brutal man-child Stanley in *A Streetcar Named Desire* (1951); Paul Newman* stepped up to the role of the surly, sozzled Brick in *Cat on a Hot Tin Roof* (1958); and the wild-eyed, self-destructive Rev. T. Lawrence Shannon from *The Night of the Iguana* (1964) was portrayed by the great Richard Burton* in one of his best film performances. Looked at another way, though, these actors all had the good fortune to be performing at a time when Williams was writing such extraordinary, unforgettable parts.

All three of those characters are distinct, original and fully formed. Yet they all have something in common, namely that they're rebelling against authority. For Stanley, that comes in the form of his sister-in-law Blanche, with her upper-class airs; for Brick, it's his plutocrat father; for Shannon, the martinet Miss Fellowes. You might further say that each rebellion seems disproportionate, like Hamlet's*. It's as if their trouble is existential, a battle with something they can't name. In Williams' case, the unnameable secret was his homosexuality, which he couldn't address on stage, his sister's schizophrenia, and his own fear of sliding into insanity. He took refuge in booze and barbiturates, exacerbated by depression as his career fell into the doldrums in the 1960s and 1970s. He killed himself in 1983.

Jackson Pollock, artist (1912–56)

A distinguished older artist once asked the American Jackson Pollock if he ever worked from nature. To which Pollock is said to have replied, 'I am nature.'

That may sound like a brutal or brattish response to a polite and quite reasonable question, and maybe that was what it was. Yet coming from Pollock, it doesn't seem entirely outlandish. In his private and professional lives, he was an irresistible force, driven by a combination of personal demons and diabolical pride. (He once declared that the only great painters of the century were Picasso, Matisse and himself.) While creating the 'drip paintings' that made him famous, he kept the canvas not vertical, as was the norm, but stretched out horizontally on the floor. Pollock would move over it restlessly, not using a paint brush but instead pouring the paint direct from the pot, or drooling and spooling it out using sticks or basting syringes. Allowing himself to be filmed at work, clad in jeans and a tight T-shirt that showed off his bulging biceps, he admitted an element of performance to his art – the artist as jazz musician – which led some to doubt the depth of his talent, as eventually would he.

Theoretical physicists specialising in chaos theory would later claim to discern fractal patterns (those that repeat on the maximal and minimal scale) in Pollock's 'drip paintings', lending a scientific authority to the artist's claim to have blurred the boundaries between art and nature. The New York art scene embraced him as a genius, an acclaim with which he was never comfortable. An alcoholic from his teens growing up in rural Wyoming, Pollock would turn up drunk to meetings with potential patrons, once staggering into a reception at the Chelsea Hotel* organised in his honour by his chief supporter, Peggy Guggenheim, and throwing up on the carpet. At the height of his success, he abandoned drip paintings. He spent his remaining years tormented by the fear that he had nothing left to say artistically, and died in a car crash, drunk at the wheel, aged 46.

Michelangelo Antonioni, film-maker (1912–2007)

What should be said about the arty Italian film-maker Michelangelo Antonioni? Firstly that if anyone ever invites you to accompany them to one of his movies, you should run in the opposite direction, shouting and waving your arms. Seriously. This was a guy who once told Jack Nicholson that for him, actors were no more important than scenery. It would have been great to have witnessed Nicholson's facial expression on hearing that one. No doubt he did one of his inimitable smiles, which would have comprehensively out-shone whatever the scenery happened to be.

What are Antonioni's films like? Like you'd expect from a director who isn't interested in actors. Very slow (albeit artis-tically shot), extremely boring and exceedingly pretentious. Notoriously, at the end of his 1962 movie *L'Eclisse*, two lovers arrange to meet on a street corner but neither bothers to turn up. So Antonioni films the empty street. For seven minutes. His characters, who tend to be played by beautiful actors, usually suffer from some kind of existential malaise that prevents them from connecting with anyone on a deep level. A point the director wanted to make, he once said, was that we live according to 'a rigid and stereotyped morality, which all of us recognise as such, and yet sustain out of cowardice and sheer laziness'. This is a pretty interesting observation – far more interesting, in fact, than anything that happens in any of his films. Antonioni's best-known work in English was 1966's *Blow-up*, in which a randy photographer (David Hemmings) gets caught up in a murder mystery. Despite the promising subject matter, it's still pretty dull.

Called on to come to Antonioni's defence, you might say that if the essence of coolness is to be simultaneously good-looking and emotionally numb (and for some, it seems, that's what it's all about), then he invented the style. Also, by framing and shooting his scenes with the scrupulous aesthetic attention of a modernist painter, he encourages the viewer to see the world with new eyes. On staggering outside after sitting through one of his films, you search your surroundings more keenly than ever for meaning, partly because you've been so starved of it in the cinema.

Jesse Owens, athlete (1913–80)

The look on Adolf Hitler's face, as the black American athlete Jesse Owens won four gold medals at the 1936 Berlin Olympics – that would have been something to see. For the Nazi leader's twisted philosophy was based on the premise that the white 'Aryan' race was supreme, a myth that was exploded by Owens' storming victories in the 100 metres, 200 metres, 100-metre relay and long jump. The story goes that the Führer was so enraged by this tour de force that he refused to shake Owens' hand. This version of events has been disputed, however. According to Owens himself, at one point their eyes met, and they waved at each other. But the Nazi armaments minister Albert Speer recalled that Hitler was 'highly annoyed' at the spectacle. He sulkily observed that, in his opinion, black athletes had an unfair physical advantage, because they were more 'primitive'. He added that it might be better if they were excluded from future competitions.

Arguably, Owens merits further admiration for refusing to toe the party line. It suited the US authorities to portray the Nazi leader as a bigot, while turning a blind eye to the racial injustices that were very much the norm back home. After winning his long jump medal, the American graciously attributed it to advice given to him by his handsome blond-haired German rival, Luz Long, in an earlier round. On returning to the US, Owens was greeted as a hero, but still treated as an inferior citizen. At a reception held to honour him at New York's Waldorf Astoria hotel, he was required to use the service elevator, so as not to share confined space with white guests. Franklin Roosevelt never sent him the customary telegram of congratulations, prompting an embittered Owens to remark, 'Hitler didn't snub me. It was our president who snubbed me.'

The reason for that omission may, at least in part, have been that Owens had been stripped of his amateur status after trying to cash in on his new-found fame. He subsequently fell into dire straits financially and was reduced to performing circus stunts to earn a crust. For instance, he would race against a horse. 'What was I supposed to do?' he demanded. 'I had four gold medals, but you can't eat four gold medals.'

Albert Camus, author (1913–60)

Philosophers don't tend to be especially cool, but the French author Albert Camus was a notable exception. He had the looks of a movie star. He wrote with such elegance and clarity (another rarity in a philosopher) that he was awarded the Nobel Prize in Literature when he was just 44. He was even a talented sportsman, keeping goal for his university football team in his native Algeria, until his athletic career was terminated by a bout of tuberculosis. And although this isn't something to be spoken of lightly, the fact that Camus died tragically young – in a car crash, at the age of 46 – helped to preserve his standing as a writer and thinker, while lending his life a glamorously doomed air in retrospect.

Camus didn't only embody continental chic by hanging out in cafés in Paris and smoking a lot of cigarettes (although he certainly did both those things). He also provided a useful philosophical underpinning for one of the key character types in the history of cool: the man who believes in nothing but ultimately does the right thing. He explored the first of these themes – the moody nihilism – in his 1942 work *The Myth of Sisyphus*, in which he suggested life could be compared to pushing a rock up a hill, knowing that when you near the top it will roll back down again. What makes this truly 'absurd' (to use Camus's favoured term) is that we all carry on behaving as if our lives have meaning, when deep down we know that they don't.

What about doing the right thing? Camus turned to this in his non-fiction work *The Rebel*. (His titles, which also include the novels *The Outsider* and *The Fall*, amount to a checklist of cool themes.) A cultural study of the figure of the 'man in revolt', the book suggests that it is only by rebelling – which by his definition involves acting for a greater good instead of only for oneself – that we force meaning and morality into an existence that would otherwise lack them. At the very least, it is in the moment of revolt that a man or woman will feel most vividly fulfilled.

William S. Burroughs, author (1914–97)

In 1951 the American author William S. Burroughs shot his wife dead. It was an accident, he said. The two were fooling around at a party in Mexico, both wasted, when he declared, 'It's time for our William Tell act.' His wife Joan obligingly placed her gin glass on her head but the trick went wrong. Burroughs narrowly avoided being convicted of murder and in the event skipped the country before he received his sentence. 'I am forced to the appalling conclusion,' he later declared, 'that I would never have become a writer but for Joan's death.'

Perhaps he was forced to that conclusion, but he wasn't forced to share it. And it's hard to resist pointing out that some people have succeeded in becoming writers without killing their spouses. From Burroughs, it was a characteristically outrageous (and, one might add, morally noxious) statement, conforming to the dominant theme of his creative life, which was the discovery of poetry in pain and a resonance in the sordid side of things. As a heroin* addict with a penchant for Maghrebian rent boys, he knew about both. And he believed in writing about what he knew: the acrid aura of authenticity is key to his appeal. The titles of his first two major works, *Junkie* and *Queer*, are explicit about their subject matter.

One of the Big Three creators of the Beatnik* movement, along with Jack Kerouac* and Allen Ginsberg*, Burroughs benefited from the endorsement of his fellow Beats. The younger Ginsberg rejected his sexual advances, but proclaimed Burroughs' 1959 novel *Naked Lunch* to be 'the masterpiece of the century'. That book is not an easy read, partly because of its content, which includes graphic descriptions of gay sex and drug-taking, and partly because Burroughs favoured a 'cut-up' approach to writing, meaning he would arrange episodes randomly. (In later works, he did likewise with the choice and order of words within sentences.) But yes, it's good. There's a dry-as-dust humour at work. And there's a rhythm to his roll through the fleshpots of New York and Tangier* (where parts of the book are set) and a sneer and drawl to his jargon, which has influenced admirers including Patti Smith* and Martin Amis.

Billie Holiday, singer (1915–59)

One night in 1939, at a nightclub named Cafe Society in New York's Greenwich Village, a black female singer stepped up to the microphone and sang a song about lynchings in the American south. What made it disturbing wasn't only the graphic imagery, but also her incongruously sleepy, almost sensual tone. The song was called 'Strange Fruit' (the title refers to the corpses of black victims dangling from poplar trees) and the singer's name was Billie Holiday: a woman who is widely regarded as one of the greatest jazz singers who ever lived.

The story of her life is the story of her voice. Untrained, it started out light and free, winging it like the jazz musicians she played with. Most notable among these was the saxophonist Lester Young, who nicknamed her 'Lady Day', an ironically aristocratic moniker for a girl who started her adult life as a prostitute and ended it a heroin* addict. In some of their greatest performances in the late 1930s, Young's bluesy playing and Holiday's blowsy voice extemporise what seems like an intimate conversation, with Young holding off in order not to interrupt Holiday's phrasing. After the cheerful show tunes of her early career, she favoured sadder-sounding ballads, which gave expression to her darker, self-destructive side. In 'My Man', she sang of being beaten by her lover, but loving him anyway. Meanwhile, her alcoholism and drug addiction were eroding her ability to sing.

After she served a nine-month term for drug possession in 1947–8 she was banned from performing in any establishments that served alcohol: an embargo that made it almost impossible for her to earn a living during the last twelve years of her life. By 1958, when she recorded her final album, *Lady in Satin*, her voice was barely there. Despite that, there are those who say the LP contains her most moving performances. She died the following year of heart and liver failure brought on by her addictions. As she lay dying, Holiday was again charged with drug possession. Her mugshot was taken. They found $750 in cash strapped to her leg. It was the only money she had in the world.

J.D. Salinger, author (1919–2010)

Romeo was a rebellious teenager. Jesus, no doubt, was a rebellious teenager. But in the decade of the rebellious teenager – which is to say, the 1950s – the one who inspired the others was a fictitious seventeen-year-old named Holden Caulfield, the hero of J.D. Salinger's slender, rambling novel *The Catcher in the Rye* (1951). The events of that book aren't the point, though for the record they include the troubled kid hanging out in the big city, getting drunk, nearly having sex with a prostitute, and generally agonising about life. The point is the voice that Salinger created for Holden. By turns slangy, sloppy, stroppy, mopey and lyrically moving, it was the most authentic and convincing voice of a rebellious teenager anyone had ever produced.

It was also, to some extent, the voice of the author. Although Salinger was 32 when his debut was published to instant acclaim, he had apparently been deep-frozen in adolescence by his wartime experiences, which included being among the first GIs into the concentration camps after the Nazi surrender. His consequent post-traumatic stress disorder (PTSD) contributed to his decision to move to an isolated New Hampshire home and become one of literary history's most notorious recluses. The consequence has been a prurient public interest in his many eccentricities. He's said, among other oddities, to have existed on a diet of peas, lamb burgers and his own urine.

Conveniently, the solitude* also preserved his reputation. If you don't fancy dying young, an alternative way to manage this trick is to keep your mouth shut and the shutters closed. Salinger continued to write, but in what has been interpreted as the ultimate act of artistic self-denial, on finishing each novel, he didn't publish it. He stashed it in a safe. 'There is a marvellous peace in not publishing,' he explained. 'It's peaceful. Still. Publishing is a terrible invasion of my privacy.'

If the PTSD diagnosis is correct, it's striking that the experience of human atrocity should have resulted in such a pitch-perfect portrayal of the trials of being a teenager. It begs the question: what is the trauma of childhood that produces the post-traumatic symptoms of adolescence? Salinger, if he had known the answer, would doubtless have kept it to himself.

Timothy Leary, psychologist (1920–96)

One day in 1957, during a trip to Mexico, a handsome Harvard psychology professor named Timothy Leary sampled hallucinogenic mushrooms for the first time. The experience, he later claimed, taught him more about human psychology in five hours than he had learnt over the previous fifteen years of his academic career. Specifically, he realised that there are realms of consciousness in the human mind that can be accessed only by certain activities. Among these are yoga, meditation, and ingesting interesting hallucinogens such as LSD* and psilocybin.

A visit to those realms, he declared, characteristically involved 'the transcendence of verbal concepts, of space-time dimensions, and of the ego or identity'. Does that mean that if you do LSD, you'll lose the ability to speak, and forget what time it is and who you are? Basically, yes. But Leary's meaning was also grander. According to him, you'll understand that words are a limiting form of expression, that space and time are fluid constructs, and that the ego is a prison. Returning to Harvard, he set up a course exploring the possible beneficial effects of psychedelic drugs, which were then legal in America. (Might criminals, for instance, be less likely to reoffend after taking LSD?) Needless to say, his curriculum proved rather popular with the students.

Abandoning Harvard, he continued his experiments, touring the country to preach the wonders of LSD. Leary famously urged people to 'turn on, tune in, and drop out'. This catchphrase – which was suggested to him by his friend, the media theorist Marshall McLuhan – roughly translates as be cool, do drugs, and don't worry too much about education or employment. It made him a guru of the counterculture, and moved President Nixon to describe him as 'the most dangerous man in America'. To Leary's dismay, his campaign had the opposite to the desired effect, leading to psychedelic drugs being banned and Leary himself getting banged up in jail. He escaped and fled the country, but was recaptured in Afghanistan.

In later life, he devoted himself to interests he summed up by the acronym SMI^2LE: space migration, intelligence increase and life extension. He toyed with the idea of being cryogenically frozen after his death. However, he opted out after deciding that cryogenicists had no sense of humour. He didn't want to 'wake up in 50 years surrounded by people with clipboards'.

Charlie Parker, musician (1920–55)

The poet Philip Larkin, a passionate jazz lover, hated the way Charlie Parker played his saxophone. He regarded him, Ezra Pound and Pablo Picasso as an evil trio who had introduced modernism into jazz, poetry and art respectively, thereby ruining them. History has only partially supported his point of view. Parker is indeed credited with introducing modernism into jazz by pioneering what became known as bebop in the 1940s: a new, artsier form of jazz, favouring frantic playing and avant-garde flourishes. But he is more generally revered as a genius. Miles Davis* once remarked that 'You can tell the history of jazz in four words. Louis Armstrong. Charlie Parker.'

Larkin's distaste isn't all that surprising, given that bebop was precisely calculated to exclude crusty white guys. Parker's fellow bebopper Thelonious Monk once confessed that 'We wanted a music that *they* couldn't play.' By 'they' he meant the white bandleaders who creamed off most of the financial reward for the virtuosity of their black musicians. The aim, then, was to develop a music so difficult only the best could play it: that was what Parker developed from his late teens, when he spent four years practising, devoting up to fifteen hours a day to what were known as 'woodshedding' sessions of intense sustained playing. This, and the music it produced, required extraordinary discipline: something Parker wasn't always able to offer. He was a heroin* addict from an early age, which made him erratic. Denied access to the drug, he would drink. He was a ladies' man.

As time went by, this lifestyle took its toll. He fell asleep during performances, or was too wasted to keep time. The novelist Ralph Ellison compared his deterioration to the spectacle of 'a man dismembering himself with a dull razor on a spotlighted stage'. Parker died of a heart attack while watching television in the hotel suite of his friend, the Baroness

Pannonica de Koenigswarter. The coroner who examined his ravaged 34-year-old body estimated his age at 53.

Jack Kerouac, author (1922–69)

Writing, like painting, has always been a physical act. What Jack Kerouac achieved, as Jackson Pollock* did with painting around the same time, was to turn it into a macho physical act. He claimed to write in marathon bursts, feeding paper into his typewriter in specially constructed 120ft reels, the better to batter away at the machine for hours on end without pausing to change paper, sustained by gulps of benzedrine, cigarettes, and bitter black coffee. He called this 'spontaneous writing' or 'kick writing', the implication being that to write could be a ride.

Its best-known product was *On the Road*, a 1957 memoir disguised as a novel, about Neal Cassady*, Allen Ginsberg* and the author travelling around America on a gap year before gap years were invented. The pseudonyms Kerouac came up with give a sense of his purpose. Cassady became Dean Moriarty (conjuring memories of Sherlock Holmes'* diabolical adversary), the saturnine guru of style; Carlo Marx (Ginsberg) suggests a comedic version of left-wing rebellion; while the name Sal Paradise (Kerouac) hints at a quest for moral grace. This last is the most overlooked aspect of the book, which is often seen as a hymn to hedonism. Yet the author himself declared that, on the contrary, it was 'a story about two Catholic buddies roaming the country in search of

God'. An athletic, alcoholic bisexual, Kerouac was obsessed with moral purity, later seeking it in Buddhism* (an exploration he described in 1958's *The Dharma Bums*).

His writing polarises opinion. Some call him a liar, because, far from being 'spontaneous', he revised his work obsessively. Or they carp that Neal Cassady was the true original, Kerouac just a follower. In the latter's defence, he admitted it. *On the Road*'s most famous passage confesses that he is always tripping along in the slipstream of the people he admires. These, he says, are:

> the mad ones, the ones who are mad to live, mad to talk, mad to be saved, desirous of everything at the same time, the ones that never yawn or say a commonplace thing, but burn, burn, burn like fabulous yellow roman candles exploding like spiders across the stars and in the middle you see the blue center-light pop and everybody goes 'Awww!'

Norman Mailer, author (1923–2007)

Norman Mailer wasn't personally all that cool, mainly because he was so keen to seem so. In the author picture that accompanied his first book, the war novel *The Naked and the Dead* (1947), he does his best impersonation of a smouldering movie idol, but ends up looking like a short, curly-haired Jewish kid, which is what he was. The reason for his inclusion here is that, in his strenuous impersonation of cool – drinking, brawling, obsessing over his personal demons and existential angst – he inadvertently provided a pastiche that helped to clarify the meaning of the word.

To be fair to Mailer, he also made an important deliberate contribution to defining the term. Like much of his writing, his 1957 essay *The White Negro* is a fog of incomprehensible nonsense, shot through with the occasional beam of insight. Cool, he argues, was invented by black Americans, before being adopted and adapted by white hipsters. It operated in the double shadow created by the horrors of the Holocaust on the one hand, and the apocalypse threatened by nuclear warfare on the other. With the past and future thus blighted, there is nothing left but to live in the present: a neat enough point, which Mailer ruins by insisting on referring to it as the search for 'orgasm'. As you read on, you realise he just really likes writing the word 'orgasm' as often as possible.

Let's not forget, too, that Mailer was at times an aggressive, drunken thug. On one occasion, he stabbed his second wife with a penknife. He then tried to make it seem cool, by writing a poem about it in which he claimed that the fact he'd attacked her with a knife, rather than a gun, proved that he still loved her a little bit. There's nothing to be said in the man's defence except that he was often surprisingly honest about his inadequacies. Finally, with *Armies of the Night* (1968) and *The Executioner's Song* (1979), he played a key role in the invention of creative non-fiction, a type of writing, also known as the New Journalism, that fed a new cool-inspired appetite for a blend of truth and creativity. Both of those books earned him Pulitzer prizes.

Marlon Brando, actor (1924–2004)

At first people said that Paul Newman* was trying to be James Dean*. And who did they say James Dean was trying to be? The answer is Marlon Brando, who arguably made the greatest single contribution of any actor to the invention of cool. The case would rest on a handful of his performances in 1950s movies, notably *A Streetcar Named Desire* (1951), *The Wild One* (1953), and *On The Waterfront* (1954). In the third, he nailed the part of the bruised loner, the beautiful loser who no matter how many times he's hit, won't stay down. Watch the second film now, and Brando looks oddly camp, snugly swathed in black leather as the leader of a riotous biker gang, but his character Johnny was the original rebel without a cause. 'What are you rebelling against?' he's asked in the movie's most often quoted moment. 'What have you got?' he replies, blending anger and indifference to form the quintessence of cool.

For my money, though, the key film is actually the first one, in which Brando played the smouldering thug Stanley Kowalski opposite Vivien Leigh's pretentious Blanche Dubois. Their wrangling scenes together showcase a clash of acting styles, with Leigh brilliantly wielding the theatrical style associated with her real-life husband Laurence Olivier, and Brando blowing her away with the force of his Method acting-inspired madness. 'Ha ha ha!' he shouts at her in an expression of brutal contempt, and he might almost have been laughing at the affectations of the thespian tradition. Brando's arrival on the scene transformed movie acting for ever with its naturalism and physicality, the new note of authenticity.

Some mocked his delivery as an incomprehensible mumble, but of course in real life people don't tend to speak with Royal Shakespeare Company clarity. In Brando's case, his lazy way of talking was partly the result of a childhood speech impediment, a mild lisp he never lost. It fitted the can't-be-bothered air of the characters he portrayed. As time went by, however, the actor, who seemed not to take much satisfaction in his abilities, really couldn't be bothered. He appeared in a string of second-rate films in the 1960s and his star waned. He then pulled off one of the great career comebacks, winning an Oscar for his majestic portrayal of a Mafia boss in *The Godfather*, and also recapturing some of the old magic in *Last Tango in Paris* and *Apocalypse Now*. After that, he lapsed into eccentricity and morbid obesity. In the last decades of his life, the one-time heart-throb topped twenty stone.

Paul Newman, actor (1925–2008)

It's tough, when you're *too* good-looking. Absurd as that sounds, it was a syndrome Paul Newman suffered from. He was one of the most handsome stars of the 20th century, a cursed blessing that led to his considerable abilities as an actor being undervalued. His looks were those of a comic book hero: fair hair, a strong jaw, piercingly blue eyes, and a hint of cruelty about the lips. As a result, he was the type who got passed over for Oscars (cf. Richard Burton*). According to the author William Goldman, Newman was a victim of his own success. He was so good at what he did, he made it look easy. People tended to assume that he wasn't really acting at all.

Newman rose to prominence playing parts that had been lined up for James Dean* before his premature death. Some sniped that he was merely a second-rate Dean (as others had said Dean was a second-rate Marlon Brando*), but he brought different qualities to the table. As the boxer Rocky Graziano in *Someone Up There Likes Me* (1958), Newman found a character type that he made his own: the man who no matter how often he's knocked down, keeps getting back up. He reprised it in *Cool Hand Luke* (1967), a film that practically constitutes a sacred text in the history of cool. In a plot that has a lot in common with that of *One Flew Over the Cuckoo's Nest*, Newman plays an irrepressible prisoner at a sadistic Florida chain gang camp, who inspires rebellious hope in his fellow inmates. In one scene he wins a game of poker* despite having a hand that contains no useful cards. 'Sometimes nothing can be a real cool hand,' he remarks, an observation that conveniently summarises the underdog creed.

Although he played his fair share of tortured rebels (for instance, in 1958's *Cat on a Hot Tin Roof* and 1961's *The Hustler*), the actor never seemed more himself than in *Butch Cassidy and the Sundance Kid* (1969), in which he was the affable, effortlessly charming Butch. This, it seems, was pretty close to his character in life. Newman was a rare example in the turbulent history of cool of a straightforwardly pleasant human being. He was noted for his long, happy marriage to the actress Joanne Woodward. When asked if he had ever been tempted to stray (and you would have to assume that he had had opportunities), he famously replied, 'Why go out for hamburgers when you have steak at home?' He is also estimated to have given away proportionately more of his wealth to charities than any other American in the 20th century.

Lenny Bruce, comedian (1925–66)

Journalists will sometimes try to tell you that 'comedy is the new rock 'n' roll', but there's nothing new about the rock-star comic. Lenny Bruce pioneered the persona in the 1950s. Having struggled early in his career with clichéd vaudevillian patter, he was reduced to playing strip joints in LA. As so often, hitting rock bottom proved a turning point. Not only did he meet his luscious future wife Honey, who was a dancer in one of the clubs, he found himself in a milieu where he had licence to do and say pretty much whatever he wanted. He began to introduce four-letter words into his comic routines, and to expatiate, improvising with his quicksilver wit, on topics that were then considered shocking. Sex, mainly. The results were filthy, fascinating, and often very funny.

'Before you're twenty,' Bruce once declared, 'you can't enjoy anything because you don't know what's going on. After you're fifty, you can't enjoy it either, because you don't have the physical energies. So you only have around twenty-five years to swing. In those twenty-five years, I'm going to swing.' If there's a better expression of the reckless, present-tense philosophy of the rock star, I don't know what it is. Note that there are actually thirty years between the ages of twenty and fifty. Bruce was so cool, he couldn't even be bothered to do the maths.

In the event, he also demonstrated by personal example one of the flaws in this approach to life: namely that if you really follow it, you may not make it to fifty. The untasted years are wasted. A handsome devil, with glamorous dark rings around his cynical eyes, Bruce had affairs and Honey left him. He refused to tailor his material to stay on the right side of the law, and was convicted of obscenity in a trial in 1964 that became a *cause célèbre*, a phrase that frequently, as in this case, means a 'cause celebrity' (Bob Dylan*, Allen Ginsberg* and Norman Mailer* were among his support-ers). Bruce became neurotic, obsessed by the idea that he was being victimised. He began to drone on about it on stage, which proved tiresome for his audience, who had been hop-ing for a good time. His paranoia was exacerbated by heroin* addiction, which killed him at the age of 41.

Richard Burton, actor (1925–84)

Laurence Olivier, widely regarded as the greatest stage actor of the 20th century, once sent a telegram to Richard Burton:

'Do you want to be a great actor or a household word?' Burton cabled back: 'Both.' It was a double ambition he undoubtedly fulfilled. The Welsh actor was known as a hell-raiser – for which read alcoholic – who enjoyed phenomenal success as a performer on stage and screen, and after marrying the gorgeous actress Elizabeth Taylor in 1964 became one half of the world's most glamorous couple. His personal charisma was such that he was envied and emulated by his peers. Asked whom he most admired as an actor, Peter O'Toole replied simply, 'Richard.' So why is Burton thought of as someone who wasted his talent?

Mainly because he's judged by the wrong criterion. Early in his career, Burton was hailed as the natural successor to Olivier, but that was never going to be his path. He was a great actor, but (unlike Olivier) a greater film star, bringing a singular, inimitable quality of rebellious intensity to his best roles, which were often angry young men, as in *Look Back in Anger*, or tortured outsiders, as in *The Spy Who Came in From the Cold* and *Night of the Iguana*. Arguably his greatest screen performance was in the film version of the comedy-drama *Who's Afraid of Virginia Woolf?*, playing a part that combined iconoclastic fervour (shaking his fist against the institution of marriage in its conventional form) with the author Edward Albee's feel for the scathing poetry of domestic strife.

'The only thing in life is language,' Burton once declared. 'Not love. Not anything else.' It's as a wielder of language that he deserves to be remembered above all, rather than as a womaniser or self-hating alcoholic (although he was also both of those things). With his rich, deep, mellifluous Welsh-accented voice, his recorded poetry readings are extra-ordinary, particularly his renditions of the stentorian verse of his compatriot Dylan Thomas. When he died of drink at the age of 58, Burton was buried with a copy of Thomas's collected works.

Allen Ginsberg, poet (1926–97)

Here are two revealing anecdotes about Allen Ginsberg. Anecdote One. When The Beatles met him at a party to cele-brate his 37th birthday, he was drunk and naked apart from his underpants, which he wore on his head. He had also hung a 'Do Not Disturb' sign on his penis. John Lennon*, it's said, was unamused and beat a hasty retreat. Anecdote Two. A couple of years later, Ginsberg, who was a communist sym-pathiser, visited Cuba, but he was deported after he described Che Guevara* as 'cute' and launched a protest against the state persecution of homosexuals.

In other words, Ginsberg was a magnificent human being. He was also an instrumental figure in the creation of the hippy counterculture. One legendary night in 1955, at the Six Gallery in San Francisco, the plump, ugly, long-haired, balding bard performed his poem *Howl* for the first time, while Jack Kerouac* hurried around filling everyone's glasses with wine. It's an extraordinary work, by turns ecstatic and naive, clichéd and original. When it was published, it sparked a furore for its graphic descriptions of gay sex, which are startling. But they're delivered with such cheerfulness – evocations of joyful screams during couplings with motorcyclists, for instance – that they also seem curiously endearing. Viewed in hindsight, the poem is a paean to the cool generation, whose pastimes and characteristics are ticked off faithfully with references to jazz, drugs*, insanity*, poverty, free love, alcohol abuse, and so on. Ginsberg even name-checks Tangier* and his sometime lover Neal Cassady*, whom he praises for his skills as a 'cocksman'.

Unofficial spokesperson for the counterculture (what other kind could there be?), the poet roamed the 1960s like a hippy Socrates*, popping up at key cultural and political events. He can be seen in the background of the film Bob Dylan* made to accompany his song 'Subterranean Homesick Blues'. He did LSD with Timothy Leary*. He took part in protests against the Vietnam war. It's generally thought that his political activism damaged the spontaneity of his verse, which was deemed to be less successful as it became more engaged. Yet he'll always be remembered and revered, not only for the lyrical manifesto of *Howl* and other invocations (e.g. *A Supermarket in California*), but also for the exuberant figure he cut: somewhere between fool and genius.

Miles Davis, musician (1926–91)

The black American jazz trumpeter Miles Davis was known as the Prince of Darkness. Part of the explanation for the nickname was that once, after an operation on his throat, he lost his temper and raised his voice, doing permanent damage to his vocal cords. As a result, when he spoke it was in a soft, saturnine whisper. It was also because of Davis's smart, smooth way of presenting himself. He was always the snappiest dresser around. But most of all, the moniker summed up two qualities critics perceived in his style of playing on classic albums such as *The Birth of the Cool* (1957), *Kind of Blue* (1959) and *Bitches Brew* (1970): a regality comprising confidence and restraint, and a 'nocturnal' quality to his small-hours sound.

Said to be the best-selling jazz record of all time, *Kind of Blue* is a good way in for beginners: relaxed but perfectionist, chilled-out but switched-on. But one of the things aficionados will tell you about Davis's greatness is that it lay in his range, the pioneering contributions he made over many decades to twitchy, experimental bebop, to so-called 'cool jazz', and later to jazz fusion as he entered his electric phase in the 1970s, when he would open for rock acts such as Neil Young and The Grateful Dead. He never looked back: an attitude he stretched to the point of refusing to play his old material. To run through the classic tracks of *Kind of Blue* would have been no more interesting, he said, than eating 'warmed-over turkey'.

When he started out, Davis's great hero was Charlie Parker*. But when he spoke of 'Bird' later it was acerbically, as 'one of the slimiest and greediest motherfuckers who ever lived'. This accusation of greed, of being a 'pig' or a 'hog', was one of Davis's preferred slurs, and it extended to personal life as well as musical style. He himself stayed always pin-thin, keeping fit by boxing after he broke his heroin* dependency of the early 1950s. There are some who have suggested this fierce disciplinarian was too controlled. The poet and jazz critic Philip Larkin, for example, carped at the 'passionless creep' of his trumpet. To others, this detachment was an integral aspect of the cool style of the inimitable Prince of Darkness.

Neal Cassady, Beatnik (1926–68)

Neal Cassady never wrote a book. He wasn't a singer-songwriter or civil-rights campaigner. Yet he has a claim to having lit the touch-paper that led to the explosion of 'cool' in the 1950s and 1960s. He managed this trick not by writing about it or acting it out, but by living it, and in such a way as to ignite the Beatnik movement, whose authors admired him as an unstoppable life force.

'He was simply a youth tremendously excited with life, and though he was a con-man, he was only conning because he wanted so much to live and to get involved with people who would otherwise pay no attention to him.' Thus, in *On the Road*, did Jack Kerouac* describe the erratic, ecstatic character of Dean Moriarty, the maverick who leads the protagonist on his existential wanderings through America. When the novel became a smash hit after its publication in 1957, readers were quick to connect Moriarty with Kerouac himself. In reality, as the author conceded, the character was based on Cassady, his fast-driving, frank-talking, free-loving proto-hipster friend.

After his mother's death when he was ten, Cassady was brought up by his alcoholic father in Colorado. He took to petty crime in his teens, served time at eighteen, and soon after, met Kerouac and Allen Ginsberg* in New York. Ill-educated as he was, he impressed both of them with his voracious appetite for reading, drinking, and sex with anyone he could get his hands on, regardless of gender. He tried writing but found it difficult. Yet his free-flowing prose, especially in an eighteen-page letter he sent Kerouac, had a huge influence on the latter's 'spontaneous writing'. Cassady could actually claim to have inspired two out of three key Beatnik* works, since Ginsberg, with whom Cassady had a long affair, dedicated his poetry collection *Howl* to 'N.C., the secret hero of these poems'.

Photographs show a handsome, strong-limbed guy, who resembled Kerouac but looked like he could take him in a fight. Also like Kerouac, Cassady had a self-destructive streak. In the 1960s he joined the tour bus of Ken Kesey's roving troupe of LSD*-toting 'Merry Pranksters'. (Some say he inspired the hero in Kesey's novel *One Flew Over the Cuckoo's Nest*.) According to his second wife Carolyn, they treated him like a 'trained bear'. He took any pill they gave him. He 'didn't care'. His body gave out when he was just 42. Cassady was found slumped by the rail tracks in the Mexican desert, having apparently decided to walk to the next town after bingeing on booze and barbiturates at a wedding party.

Michel Foucault, author (1926–84)

While on holiday in Italy with his boyfriend Jean, the shaven-headed, turtleneck-sweater-sporting French philosopher Michel Foucault stumbled on a collection of essays that changed his life. In them, Friedrich Nietzsche argued that the purpose of studying history was not to understand the past, but to get to grips with the present. Foucault interpreted this to mean that history should be used as a weapon. His targeted areas were chosen according to personal taste. A promiscuous homosexual with a weakness (or perhaps that should be a strength) for sadomasochism, Foucault focused on defending those whom society regarded as insane, or criminal, or sexually deviant.

His usual method was to argue that, contrary to popular belief, the way such people had been treated in the past was actually far more humane than in his own day. In *Madness and Civilisation* (1960), for example, Foucault pointed out that those deemed 'mad' had been tolerated and even valued as special in certain societies at certain times, permitted to co-exist alongside the sane. In his era, when lobotomies and electro-shock therapy were common psychiatric practices, Foucault's argument that there was something to be learnt from the past carried a certain force.

However, when he attempted a similar manoeuvre with the justice system in *Discipline and Punish* (1975), he found himself forced to resort to more tortuous theorising, to be highly selective in his use of examples, and often, his critics said, deliberately to misinterpret them. Ditto when he explored ideas of sexual normalcy in his hefty, unfinished *History of Sexuality*.

A classic example of Foucault getting it wrong came when he suggested that the AIDS virus was a fiction invented by the authorities to oppress the gay community. In due course he contracted the disease, which killed him. To this day, he is a theorist popular with angry young intellectuals. For in order to do battle with the establishment, you first have to be convinced that it's worth doing battle with, and for this project Foucault provides useful machinery. More generally, his suggestion that all presumptions, but particularly the presumption of progress, should be relentlessly re-examined, remains influential, not only because it's radical, but also because it's right.

Che Guevara, revolutionary (1928–67)

What on earth did Che Guevara, who was from Argentina, think he was doing, fighting a guerrilla war in Cuba? It's as if, say, an Englishman were to go off and fight for Greek independence (which actually some, such as Lord Byron*, did). The explanation is that from an early age, Guevara viewed all South American countries as a single entity, victimised by the imperialist oppression of the USA. This perception came to him during an epic motorbike journey he undertook through the continent. He was particularly appalled by the grim conditions he saw endured by the workers in a Chilean copper mine. He vowed that he would dedicate his life to helping all those who were similarly exploited, by armed revolution if necessary.

His chance came after a meeting with Fidel Castro, who was plotting the overthrow of the US-backed Cuban dictator Fulgencio Batista. Together they waged a guerrilla campaign from Cuba's Sierra Maestra mountains, which ended in total victory in 1959. In war, Guevara proved both brave and ruthless. After carrying out his first execution, he recorded the details of the wound in his diary, and his own lack of remorse, with a forensic satisfaction bordering on relish. His extreme Marxist convictions later caused tensions between himself and the more cautious Castro, who sent Guevara on a mission to spread revolution in other countries. The latter's luck finally ran out in Bolivia, where he was captured and summarily shot by CIA-assisted Bolivian forces.

Guevara owes much of his iconic status to a particular photo, which is said to have been reproduced more often than any other photograph in history. The so-called *Guerrillero Heroico*, which was snapped at a state funeral by Castro's official photographer Alberto Korda, shows the revolutionary leader in a military beret, his handsome features stern, framed by his dark, unkempt curls. The image has adorned so many student bedrooms as to have lost almost all meaning, except to proclaim adherence to some vague anti-establishment philosophy.

In his lifetime, Guevara also enjoyed the admiration of left-wing thinkers. The French existential philosopher Jean-Paul Sartre, for example, was present when the

Guerrillero Heroico was taken. He once rather grandly described Guevara as 'the most complete human being of our time'.

Andy Warhol, artist (1928—87)

The meaning of cool is constantly shifting, for as soon as one version of it gains general acceptance, it gives birth to the possibility of another version. For example, after abstract expressionist painters such as Jackson Pollock* made tortured self-expression the height of fashion in New York in the 1950s, it ceased to be daring. It seemed more daring *not* to be tortured, or at least not to reveal it, and if possible to remove yourself as far as possible from the creation of the artwork. Enter Andy Warhol, the priest of detachment and prophet of pop art commercialism.

Like an artistic Oscar Wilde, the homosexual Warhol forged a name for himself by inverting expectations. He made no secret of his interest in wealth, coolness and fame (once optimistically declaring that in the future everyone would be famous for fifteen minutes), precisely because these were the very things to which a true artist was supposed to be indifferent. One thing Warhol wasn't indifferent about was sustaining his pose of indifference, which he wore like a suit of armour. He was notoriously uncommunicative in interviews, preferring to respond in monosyllables. Banality and passivity were his weapons, sometimes to the point of self-parody. As the Velvet Underground singer Lou Reed*, whose early career Warhol sponsored, once observed, 'They should make a doll of Andy Warhol: one that you wind up and it doesn't do anything.'

Warhol's masterstroke was to suggest his passivity was profound, his absence declaring his presence. This implication was machine-tooled to stimulate debate, as were the works that embodied it. Were his screen prints of celebrities such as Marilyn Monroe, Elvis Presley* and Muhammad Ali*, their faces portrayed in lurid, clownish, psychedelic colours, a con trick or a serious comment? And how about his avant-garde films such as *Sleep* (which showed one of his friends sleeping), *Eat* (which showed one of his friends eating) and *Blow Job* (you get the idea)? You may not like the mood or motives of his art but you have to acknowledge its impact, and his affectless Machiavellianism. In an interview in 1980, Warhol described himself as a virgin, which led to a general perception that he was asexual. The testimony of his boyfriends contradicts this, so why did he take the trouble to claim it? At least partly, it was because he understood that, in an era when promiscuity was thought to be cool, the only thing that might possibly be considered cooler was its opposite.

Maya Angelou, author (1928–2014)

When Maya Angelou was eight years old, she was raped by her mother's boyfriend. She told her brother, who told her uncles, and the man was beaten to death. Convinced it was somehow her voice that had killed him, the girl didn't speak again for five years. Instead she read, devouring the works of canonical white authors such as Dickens and Shakespeare and black female authors such as Frances Harper, a self-administered education that would ultimately propel her own emergence as a literary artist. Angelou's lyrical, strikingly immediate autobiographical volumes, which began in 1969 with *I Know Why The Caged Bird Sings*, benefited from the perception that her personal story was, on some level, a representative African American narrative.

Although critics disputed some details of her accounts, she possessed the authentic air of one who had lived many lives. Throughout her descriptions of her experiences as a waitress, prostitute, brothel madam, singer, bus conductress, actress, black activist, dancer and journalist, a moving tension accumulates in the knowledge that her day in the sun, when she will be feted as a role model, is approaching. This need to wait, and the ability to do so, manifested also in her approach to writing. She used to check into a hotel room, remove the pictures from the walls so she wouldn't be distracted, have a couple of nips of sherry, and then sit down with a deck of cards and play patience until she felt ready to put pen to paper.

As well as a memoirist, she was an acclaimed poet, whose 1971 volume *Just Give Me a Cool Drink of Water 'fore I Diiie* was nominated for a Pulitzer Prize. Perhaps her best-loved poem, *Still I Rise*, is a classic expression of the trope of the rebel who won't submit to oppression. Its message is that however often and hard you put her down, she'll just keep getting back up. There were those who detected a self-congratulatory note in some of her later work, platitudes in her verse, and a cheapening eye for business. (Her name appeared on pillows, mugs and greetings cards.) To this last accusation, Angelou's attitude was cheerfully unrepentant. 'I agree,' she declared, 'with Balzac and 19th-century writers, black and white, who say, "I write for money."'

Jean-Luc Godard, film-maker (b. 1930)

It's amazing how uncool French rock music can be. Often, it's excruciating, mainly because it tries so hard to sound like American rock music. By contrast, when a group of young French film-makers at the end of the 1950s set out to create films that were glaring tributes to American genre flicks, they succeeded spectacularly. The revolutionary films of the Nouvelle Vague (New Wave) embodied a uniquely French form of dispassionate coolness. And none was cooler than the handful made by Jean-Luc Godard at the start of his long, and still ongoing, career.

The most obvious example is his thrilling debut, 1960's À Bout de souffle (known to English-speaking audiences as Breathless), which he made on a shoestring budget, relying heavily on improvisation and scribbling scenes on the hoof. There's a scene in which the young hoodlum protagonist (Jean-Paul Belmondo) gazes admiringly at a poster of Humphrey Bogart* and tries to imitate his expression: a pretty flagrant confession by the director of what he was up to. In fact, Godard may be making a similar point at the end of the film, when the hero gets shot owing to the treachery of his shallow American girlfriend (Jean Seberg). Even the coolest French dude is no match for an ordinary American chick, he seems to say. At the same time, he was staking out new territory with his conjunction of existential nihilism and formal experimentation. 'A story,' he once remarked, 'should have a beginning, a middle and an end, but not necessarily in that order.'

Godard continued to experiment, using Brechtian techniques to remind the audience that they were watching a film, in movies such as *Pierrot le fou* (1965) and *Week-end* (1967). The following year saw the release of *Sympathy for the Devil*, which interspersed intriguing footage of the Rolling Stones in the studio composing the eponymous song with baffling scenes in which revolutionaries from the Black Panther movement shout slogans. He wanted to call the film *1 + 1*, and when the producer changed it to the more commercially viable title under which it was released, Godard punched him in the mouth. He should probably have listened to the guy. With the passing of time, his movies became more politically preachy and his audience drifted away.

James Dean, actor (1931–55)

If you were writing a book about cool (let's imagine this, just for the sake of argument), and required one face to adorn the cover, James Dean's would be an obvious choice. He is probably the number one cool icon of all time. How did this happen? After all, this is a guy who only ever made three movies, before dying in a car crash at the age of 24. Part of the answer must be that his premature death was the photographic fixer that set his image in the mind of the public: a talent that was frozen for ever at the start of his career, when his promise was still limitless.

The received wisdom is that his performances in those films – *East of Eden* (1955), *Rebel Without a Cause* (1955), and *Giant* (1956) – were electrifying (he was Oscar-nominated for the first and third). Dean studied Method* acting at New York's Actors Studio. Method was all about truth. His acting, it's said, was a newer, truer style. But come to it today, and he seems merely to have found a new way to be unrealistic. He was good. But all the pouting and shouting and moue-mouthed emoting haven't aged particularly well (by comparison with some of Marlon Brando's* work in the same decade, for instance). Perhaps this doesn't matter, since most people now don't take the trouble to watch Dean's films. They just absorb that image, the face, the style, the pose, the way he wore his clothes, a cigarette clamped between soft lips, his collar turned up against a bitter existential wind. When it comes to James Dean, it's all about the look.

The 2015 movie *Life*, which focuses on the friendship between the actor and the *Life* magazine photographer Dennis Stock, convincingly suggests that the Dean legend is rooted in a handful of key images. His face was far more feminine than those of most previous male Hollywood idols, carrying an appeal not only for women but also for gay men, who have tended to embrace the theory, for which there is a certain amount of evidence, that Dean was homosexual. Above all, his face was young. It was the face of a teenager or even a child (with a hint of the cadaver in the sunken eyes and slanted cheek bones). Yet the characters he played were wise beyond their years. Or to be precise, they had a special wisdom that adults couldn't understand. That was what was revolutionary about Dean's unspoken but articulate message: this idea that the young knew something that the old didn't and couldn't.

Dean liked to say that he wanted to 'live fast, die young and leave a beautiful corpse'*. He managed two out of three. As it happened, the actor had shaved back his hairline to play the final scenes of *Giant*, in which his character was in his sixties. So by a curious quirk of fate, when he met death, the embodiment of rebellious youth looked decades older than he was.

Guy Debord, author (1931–94)

Guy Debord liked to claim that there was no such thing as reality any more. There was only what he referred to as the Spectacle: a hypnotic but profoundly false display created by capitalist forces with the connivance of our own psychological flaws (for instance, our pathetic fondness for being entertained). In his best-known work, 1967's *La Société du spectacle*, Debord argued that this syndrome had overwhelmed every aspect of our lives, down to our most intimate private moments, making direct experience practically impossible. All of which begs the response: wasn't he rather overstating things? Clearly he was on to something in his excoriation of the insidious influence of advertising (whose power has grown with the advent of the internet). But the way he wrote about it, he made it sound as if we were all trapped in some nightmarish sci-fi scenario, helpless slaves of an evil, invisible matrix of artificiality.

Debord did, however, succeed in getting people's attention, which, on some level, was his aim. He was a leading member of the Situationist movement, a post-Surrealist group devoted to shocking people out of their complacency by creating startling 'situations' designed to give them a jolt. One of Debord's co-conspirators, for example, once slipped into Notre Dame cathedral disguised as a priest, commandeered the pulpit, and announced to the horrified congregation that God had died. Debord himself came up with the amusing gimmick of publishing his first book, *Mémoires*, with a cover made of rough sandpaper, so it would damage any other book it was placed next to on a bookshelf. He later directed a film entitled *Hurlements en faveur de Sade* (Howls for Sade), which showed a screen that was either entirely white or entirely black, depending on whether there was any dialogue playing on the soundtrack. The movie ended with 24 minutes of black-screen silence. (Cf. the ending of *L'Eclisse* by Michelangelo Antonioni*, which makes a similar joke.)

The Situationist philosopher achieved a certain cachet in 1968, when student rioters in Paris borrowed phrases from

La Société du spectacle and shouted them as slogans. To this day, he remains popular with left-wing intellectual types. The comedian Russell Brand, for example, is a fan. Debord committed suicide at the age of 63 by shooting himself in the heart.

Miriam Makeba, singer (1932–2008)

Miriam Makeba was the first African singer to enjoy chart success in the US and the first African woman to win a Grammy award. Extremely beautiful, with a rich, clear voice that critics compared to that of Ella Fitzgerald, the South African was seen as an ambassador not only for her country but also for her continent. In this capacity, her nicknames included Mama Africa. To judge the resonance of this, and its orientalist absurdity, consider which American singer, if any, might reasonably be referred to as Mrs America.

Names seem to have dogged the singer's life. She was born Zenzile Miriam Makeba in Prospect Township on the outskirts of Johannesburg. Her first name was derived from a word in her father's Xhosa language meaning 'You have only yourself to blame'. Apparently, this was meant to ward off bad luck, but if so it didn't work. When Makeba was six days old, her mother, a traditional healer, was imprisoned for illegally brewing beer, with the result that the child spent the first six months of her life in jail. In early adulthood she decided that music was 'a type of magic' that could transform her life. And so it proved. Having made a name for herself as a singer in her native land, in 1959 she travelled to the Venice Film Festival to attend the screening of an anti-apartheid documentary* in which she made a cameo appearance. From here, she continued to the US, where she was instantly acclaimed as a star.

Her biggest hits, which included the infectious 'Pata Pata' and 'The Click Song', were her earliest. To her delight, Makeba found herself befriended by celebrities such as the actor Marlon Brando* and the singer Harry Belafonte. She even performed at JFK's birthday, where she shared the billing with Marilyn Monroe. But the singer's happiness was blighted by the discovery that she had been banned from returning to South Africa owing to her opposition to apartheid. In exile, she threw her energies into supporting the civil rights campaign and later the black power movement, whose controversial leader Stokely Carmichael she married in 1968. Makeba was among those who performed at the Rumble in the Jungle boxing match between George Foreman and Muhammad Ali* in Zaire in 1974. In 1987 she accompanied the singer Paul Simon on his Gracelands tour. Notwithstanding her involvement in these highly politicised events, she always denied that she was a political singer. 'What I sing is not politics,' she declared. 'It is the truth.'

Ronald Kray, criminal (1933–95), & Reginald Kray, criminal (1933–2000)

What was cool about the Kray twins? They were relatively small-time East End thugs, multiple murderers, and, at least in the case of Ronnie, certifiably insane. By its nature, criminality balances recklessness against ingenuity, and expresses a desire for freedom so desperate it runs the risk of losing it. So far, so cool – but no further. Beyond that point, the value system of the Krays is a perverse and perverted image of the cool philosophy. It is cool's portrait in the attic.

Nevertheless, people continue to misidentify the Krays as cool, a confusion they encouraged. Inspired by the Soho gangster* Billy Hill (who was himself said to have based his personal style on that of Humphrey Bogart*), they set themselves up as respectable-seeming nightclub owners with the money they collected from protection rackets and other scams. Among their celebrity friends were the Hollywood actor George Raft, who had starred in the original version of the gangster movie *Scarface*, the actress Barbara Windsor, and the celebrity photographer David Bailey*.

Their own identification as celebrities was a key aspect of their image. At one point in their 1969 trial, Ronnie proudly informed the startled judge, 'If I wasn't here, I could be having tea with Judy Garland.' Acutely aware of the importance of being written about, in 1967 they invited the author John Pearson, who had just published a biography of James Bond* author Ian Fleming, to write a book focusing on their philanthropy. In the event, his gripping work *The Profession of Violence* (1972) concentrated on their villainy. While purporting to decry their legend, it cemented it.

Since then there have been more than fifty books written about this interchangeable pair of psychotic idiots and a handful of high-profile movies that seek to glamorise them. But consider first Pearson's almost unreadably gruesome account of their murder of their associate Jack 'The Hat' McVitie, who had bungled a job they'd given him. Arriving in an apartment in Stoke Newington, he finds the terrible twins waiting for him. When Reggie points a gun at him, it jams. Jack tries to escape through a window but gets stuck. They drag him back into the room. Ronnie holds him down and Reggie stabs him below the eye and then repeatedly in the stomach until his liver spills out. Then consider this. Reggie claimed to have found God in prison. In 1991, he published a slim volume of his reflections entitled *Thoughts*. Eventually, he said, he would like to be remembered not as a multiple murderer but as an 'author, poet and philosopher'. Does that sound cool?

Nina Simone, singer (1933–2003)

At New York's Carnegie Hall in 1964, Nina Simone introduced the next song. 'The name of this tune,' she said, 'is "Mississippi Goddam".' The swish white audience tittered, since in those days 'goddam' was a rude word. 'And I mean every word of it,' the singer added, which provoked more titters. Simone then launched into a protest song, which she'd written in response to the bombing of an Alabama church by white supremacists. Later in the performance, she interjected, 'I bet you thought I was kidding, didn't you?' By now, they realised she wasn't, and no one laughed.

An ugly duckling, Simone became a swan when she sang. Yet she'd never wanted that to be her profession. Her dream had been to be a classical pianist and with this in mind she spent years in laborious training before being rejected by the prestigious Curtis Institute in Philadelphia – for reasons of race, she was convinced. Simone began playing piano in a bar to make ends meet, performing jazz, blues, show tunes, whatever she knew. The owner insisted she sing too, and thus, against her will, her career was launched. For it turned out that Simone had a fantastic voice: a deep, smoky, unmistakable timbre, which seemed to suggest the memory of suffering swept aside by the energy of the moment, and the beat and swing of the music.

'Sinnerman'. 'Feeling Good'. 'I Put A Spell On You'. 'My Baby Just Cares For Me'. The list of indispensable Simone songs is long and distinguished. But as time went by, she increasingly channelled her energies into the civil rights movement, a cause she embraced with aggressive commitment. Her first words to Martin Luther King were, 'I'm not non-violent.' Violence had always been a part of her life: racist violence, the violence she suffered from her husband Andy (who she said raped her on the day they got engaged), and the violence she meted out in turn on her daughter.

Her mood swings and politics sabotaged her career. She emigrated, first to Africa, and then to Paris where she sang to audiences who barely remembered who she was. Only late in life was she diagnosed as bipolar. Simone had always been a geek: the shy girl who would have preferred just to play the piano. When she danced, her movements were endearingly awkward. But she was a mesmerising performer. Once she angrily told a group of music executives, 'I am a genius! I am not a clown!' The surviving footage of her concerts suggests she may have had a point.

Gloria Steinem, writer (b. 1934)

No one has a perfectly symmetrical face. But if you look in the mirror, the face that stares back seems to be fairly evenly balanced. The explanation for this is that your brain, which logically believes faces to be symmetrical, automatically adjusts what you see, distorting your vision so your face looks undistorted. Which begs the question: what else might seem symmetrical, because it's more convenient to see it that way? One answer, if you're a man, is the state of gender equality in the western world. The convenient thing is to see it as kind of symmetrical. As relatively balanced. To say: OK, maybe things aren't perfect for women, but we've come so far. Surely there's little left to do. Or little of any real urgency. Right?

Wrong, according to the American journalist and author Gloria Steinem. By her account, feminism has operated in two waves, each of roughly a hundred years. The first of these ended with the successes of the Suffragettes at the start of the 20th century. Second-wave feminism, which began in the late 1960s, is only half done, says Steinem, who has been one of its most devoted contributors. As it happens, she herself has an almost perfectly symmetrical face. In other words, she is beautiful, an accident she has used to her advantage in her quest to demonstrate to our still male-dominated society its own convenient blindness. It was thanks to her looks that, early in her career, she got a job as a Playboy Bunny at New York's Penthouse Club, so she could write an exposé of the rampant sexism at the heart of that queasy institution. And any man who complained she was taking things too seriously would be asked first to don the bunny ears and tail.

This sleight of mind was what, in a 1984 article, the novelist Martin Amis referred to as one of Steinem's main 'dialectical techniques'. In short, she asks men how *they* would like it. In one entertaining essay, she hypothesised a world in which men menstruated, and concluded that they would brag to each other about their degree of suffering, or try to make the cycle seem cool. ('Man, you lookin' *good*!' 'Yeah, man, I'm on the rag!' etc.) Steinem's sporadic introduction of humour into her sermons has made *her* seem cool – as has her continued commitment to the cause, touring and lecturing despite suffering chronic performance anxiety (which she somehow disguises) and abusive responses, and on into what is now her eighth decade.

Elvis Presley, singer (1935–77)

It's a little hard now to understand why pubescent fans went sex-crazy over The Beatles. In the case of Elvis Presley, it makes immediate sense. The King of Rock 'n' Roll, as he later came to be known, was ridiculously good-looking, with a sloppy grin, darkly feminine eyes, and a thick, slicked quiff of ink-black hair. In addition to which, the way he danced when he sang his songs was practically pornographic. However much he may have denied it (as he felt forced to, in the face of the moralistic horror that greeted his rise to prominence), the sleazily athletic jerk and sling of his hips was erotic in the most literal sense. No wonder the girls screamed and clawed their hair.

None of which is to detract from Elvis's achievements as what critics call an 'interpreter of song' (meaning he didn't write his own stuff). The blend of his looks, his louche stage presence and strong, high-baritone voice made him the most successful solo singer of all time. Add to this the fact that, as a pretty white boy with a knack for outsider music, who introduced the pain of the blues to the aw-shucks ease of country music, he embodied – even more than James Dean*, say – the breakthrough of 'cool' style into the mainstream. And Elvis somehow managed all this without losing his air of being a decent, straightforward country boy from Mississippi, and one who, most of the time, just seemed to be having fun. In interviews, he came across as sharp and grounded. If anyone could handle unprecedented levels of fame, surely it was Elvis?

As it turned out, not. His legend has been strengthened by its tragic arc: from paragon to parody, and finally to parable. The one-time sex symbol became a caricature of excess, addicted to Cadillacs, bacon-and-banana butties, and prescription medication. He took pills to sleep, pills to perform, pills to go to the loo. Near the end, he gave a performance in Las Vegas of his ballad 'Are You Lonesome Tonight?' Obese, exhausted, heavily perspiring, and wired on drugs, Elvis forgets the lyrics. He amuses himself improvising some alternative words, but there's fear in his eyes, and such tiredness. He was found dead at the age of 42 at his ranch in rural Tennessee, slumped in the bathroom, killed by a cocktail of causes brought on by his prescription drug abuse.

Dick Cavett, talk show host (b. 1936)

Jimi Hendrix*. Janis Joplin*. David Bowie*. John Lennon*. Jean-Luc Godard*. Tennessee Williams*. Marlon Brando*. Richard Burton*. Miles Davis*. Maya Angelou*. Muhammad Ali*. These are just some of the famous names who appeared on ABC's *Dick Cavett Show* during that programme's heyday between 1968 and 1974 – which, when it comes to the history of cool, was a useful heyday to have. Something of a cool cat himself, in a quiet, understated way, the slim, handsome, self-effacing presenter neither patronised nor attempted to out-cool his interviewees. He just seemed interested. As a result, they relaxed, and those televised conversations are in many cases among the most revealing footage we have of them.

Dick Cavett always had the air of a talented understudy presenter, filling in for the real star who was off sick. But that was what made him a star. Unlike some of his rivals, he didn't seem in love with the sound of his own voice. Yet his was a voice worth listening to: a rich, velvety baritone that seemed surprising from such a relatively small man. He deployed it with a wit that he had honed writing jokes for other presenters. (It was Cavett who came up with the perfect line to introduce the famously buxom actress Jayne Mansfield: 'And here they are, Jayne Mansfield!') He had also hardened his skills on the stand-up circuit. Sample gag: 'I went to a Chinese-German restaurant. The food is great, but an hour later you're hungry for power.'

Owing to his self-deprecating manner, Cavett was sometimes underestimated by his guests, although they did so at their peril. There was the time the pugnacious novelist Norman Mailer* was on the show, lined up against his fellow author and arch rival Gore Vidal, with Cavett as mediator. Mailer, who was drunk, rudely declared himself the intellectual superior of everyone present. This annoyed Cavett, who asked Mailer if he would like two extra chairs to house his 'giant intellect'. To which Mailer replied: 'Why don't you look at your question sheet and ask your question?' Cavett, after a pause: 'Why don't you fold it five ways and put it where the moon don't shine?' Mailer: 'Did you come up with that line yourself?' Cavett: 'I have to tell *you* a quote from Tolstoy?' Mailer may have had the larger intellect, but when it came to repartee, Cavett was king.

Hunter S. Thompson, author (1937–2005)

Hunter S. Thompson once visited Ernest Hemingway's* log cabin in Idaho and filched a pair of elk antlers that hung above the front door. His whole career was, in a manner of speaking, a prank carried out at the older author's expense. He idolised Hemingway, once typing out the entirety of his novel *A Farewell to Arms*, just to learn how it felt to write a masterpiece. Yet his approach to writing couldn't have been more different. For Hemingway made a name for himself by introducing the simplicity and directness of journalism into the novel. Thompson did the opposite. He took the qualities most associated with novel-writing (stylistic flourishes, for instance, and flagrant subjectivity) and injected them into his non-fiction.

In its first phase – as it was practised by Thompson in his 1966 book about the Hell's Angels, and by other authors such as Norman Mailer* and Tom Wolfe – this approach was dubbed the New Journalism. Thompson being Thompson, he took it further, spawning the offshoot known as Gonzo Journalism. It was similar but crazier. The flourishes were more flamboyant, the distinction between truth and fiction blurred beyond recognition, and it really was almost all about the author. The best-known product was Thompson's 1971 book *Fear and Loathing in Las Vegas*, which is a work of comic genius. A fictionalised non-fiction account of a road trip through the Nevada desert fuelled by a mind-boggling array of illegal drugs, the story draws strength from one principal joke. This was the miracle that the author was able to write at all if he had really ingested as many mind-altering stimulants as he claimed. It was the joke behind a lot of Thompson's writing and it remained funny for as long as he could pull it off. But it proved an increasingly tough one to sustain.

In 1974, *Rolling Stone* magazine sent him to Zaire to cover the Rumble in the Jungle boxing match between George Foreman and Muhammad Ali*. Thompson showed up but got drunk in his hotel and missed the fight. After that, he just couldn't keep it together enough to write as well as he had – or often, to write at all. Like Hemingway before him, he succumbed to the pressure to live up to the expectations people had of him in the flesh. He always had to act like Hunter S. Thompson, while nursing the painful awareness that he could no longer write like him. He eventually killed himself at his home in Colorado at the age of 68. His son, in the next room, thought the gunshot was the sound of a book falling from a shelf.

Robert Fraser, gallery owner (1937–86), & Christopher Gibbs, antiques dealer (b. 1938)

Neither Robert Fraser nor Christopher Gibbs quite deserves an entry to himself. Yet taken together, as the reputed inventors of Swinging London*, and 'style gurus' (to use Mick Jagger's phrase) to their friends the Rolling Stones and The Beatles, they have as great a claim as anyone to have made a substantial contribution to the meaning of the word cool.

Known as 'Groovy Bob', Fraser owned a gallery in Mayfair that specialised in avant-garde artists such as Peter Blake and Richard Hamilton. Gibbs, who was sometimes referred to as 'the king of Chelsea', was an antiques dealer with a line in bohemian chic. Both men were homosexual, Eton-educated, drug-toting aristocrats who impressed the new generation of working-class rock stars with their blend of artistic taste and louche *savoir vivre*. It was Fraser who recommended Blake as the artist to design The Beatles' cover for their *Sergeant Pepper* album. Gibbs is credited as the set designer on the art-house movie *Performance*, in which Jagger played a decadent rock star and romped in a bed with Anita Pallenberg*.

When the police raided Keith Richards'* country house Redlands in 1967, both Gibbs and Fraser were among the group that got busted. Hamilton's painting *Swingeing London* was based on a photograph that showed Jagger and Fraser handcuffed in a police van, covering their faces from the paparazzi. In the trial that followed, Fraser claimed that the drugs found at the house had all been his, and got six months' hard labour for his pains.

'It's easy to become a legend,' he once observed. 'All you have to do is give something up when you're at the top of your game.' He ditched his gallery soon afterwards and disappeared to India for five years. Returning to London, he set up a new gallery in the 1980s that promoted artworks by the likes of Jean-Michel Basquiat and Keith Haring. He died of AIDS aged 49. Gibbs, who with his flowery shirts and flared trousers had pioneered the look of the 'peacock dandy', was forced to sell his family home in Oxfordshire in 2000. He now lives in Tangier*, where according to a friend he has four houses, 'moving from one to the other as the mood takes him'.

David Bailey, photographer (b. 1938)

'The best way to get their knickers off is to make them laugh.' Thus does the photographer David Bailey explain his success with the opposite sex. The normal reaction on hearing someone declare what a great sense of humour they have is to doubt it. But in Bailey's case, he may actually be telling the truth, since the number of beautiful women he has stepped out with over the years is pretty dazzling. They include the models Jean Shrimpton and Penelope Tree, and the actress Catherine Deneuve, whom he married in 1965, with Mick Jagger in attendance as best man.

It may have helped his cause that, back in the day, Bailey was as good-looking as the celebrities he photographed. He was talented too, had the edgy appeal of his working-class background, and in addition wielded a power that was peculiar to his profession. As the most famous photographer of the famous, he could make you famous by photographing you. Having established his reputation working for *Vogue* magazine, in 1964 he brought out *Pin-Ups*, a definitive box of poster-prints of those he deemed to be the coolest celebrities of the day. These included The Beatles, Mick Jagger, Andy Warhol*, and the psychotic gangsters*, Ronnie and Reggie Kray*, who were from the same part of London's East End as Bailey.

The photographer's father had a scar on his face that he'd reportedly received from Ronnie Kray, but Bailey didn't bear a grudge. A vegetarian from an early age, with a lifelong passion for ornithology, he had never really got on with his dad, who used to say he thought his boy was probably 'queer'. Bailey's choice of career seems to have been calculated to annoy him. Others, though, would be more impressed by his talents. The trendy Italian film-maker Michelangelo Antonioni* based the stylish hero of his film *Blow-up* on Bailey. Reggie Kray, at whose wedding he was official photographer, once revealed that he envied him. 'Dave,' he declared morosely, 'I wish I could have done it legit like you.'

As for Bailey himself, he doesn't seem particularly bothered that one of his former clients was a multiple murderer. 'Terrible people,' he observed cheerfully of the Krays. 'But politicians are terrible people too.' This lightness of touch has always been among his qualities. Once, he said, a fan wrote to him agonising over the existential questions of life. What did it all mean? What, in the end, was the point? Bailey wrote back, advising simply, 'Make the best of it, mate, because that's all you've got.'

John Lennon, singer and songwriter (1940–80)

The Beatles may have seemed like a bunch of nice lads from Liverpool but they always had a revolutionary edge. 'For our last number, I'd like to ask your help,' the singer John Lennon declared at the 1963 Royal Variety Performance in the presence of Princess Margaret. 'For the people in the cheaper seats, clap your hands. And the rest of you, if you'd just rattle your jewellery.' (He'd originally planned on saying 'your f***ing jewellery', but been talked out of it by his manager,

Brian Epstein.) He was a funny guy, Lennon, but not always an easy man.

Thin-lipped, thin-skinned, and with tightly flared nostrils that always made it look like he was on the point of losing his temper, he joined forces with Paul McCartney, George Harrison and Ringo Starr to form the most successful pop band in history. But Lennon was always the smartest, the one worth listening to. It was he who observed, in a conversation with an English journalist about the decline in religion, that The Beatles were 'more popular than Jesus'. The remark was taken out of context by po-faced Americans as a confession of a Messianic complex, which led to general outrage and protests from the Ku Klux Klan (proof The Beatles were doing something right). Then, as luck would have it, Lennon underwent a personal transformation that made it look as if the Americans might have had a point.

He fell in love with a pretentious artist named Yoko Ono, left his wife and The Beatles, grew his hair long, and preached peace on earth. Suddenly, he looked like Jesus. Equally, though, he looked like Ono. He even adopted her name, becoming John Ono Lennon. Their private life became a public series of 'happenings', such as their 'bed-in' for peace on their honeymoon, when they held court to journalists from their marital bed as an arty anti-war statement. It was an unforeseeable plot twist in Lennon's trajectory from mop-top performer to boho protestor, which, with the benefit of hindsight, is as integral to his legend as Elvis Presley's* later decline was to his. Yet in Lennon's case, there was no decline.

He was engaged in the pursuit of happiness and appeared to be on course for finding it.

Compared with some of his Beatles classics, the songs of his solo career were a bit on-the-nose. The titles – 'Jealous Guy', 'Cold Turkey' – tended to say it all. Honesty, though, was what Lennon was all about. The hardest twist came in the manner of his death, killed by a gunman who, after reading J.D. Salinger's* *The Catcher in the Rye*, identified Lennon as an example of the kind of 'phoney' loathed by that book's teenage hero. The gunman was a madman. Lennon may sometimes have been a fool, but he was no phoney.

Bob Dylan, singer and songwriter (b. 1941)

A lot of rock stars you can love, but you can't, ultimately, take them all that seriously. Bob Dylan you can. His is a body of work that bears comparison with that of a great novelist or poet. Which was what, early in his career, he aspired to be. Shrugging off his given name of Robert Zimmerman, this short Jewish kid from Minnesota travelled to New York as a Beatnik* troubadour* in the biting cold January of 1961 and began performing in Greenwich Village cafés as Bob Dylan. The choice of surname is widely thought to have been a doffing of his then-habitual Dutch Boy cap to the poet Dylan Thomas.

His voice was a shock from the start: something between a buzz saw and the whine of his own harmonica. When Bobby Womack heard it, he said he didn't get it, until his friend Sam Cooke explained that from now on, it wasn't going to be about how pretty your voice was. It was going to be about whether people believed you were telling the truth. The implication was that in Dylan's case, the rawness of the voice was essential to his air of authenticity: there was little left to do but listen to the lyrics. He was embraced by right-on lefties as a rebel 'protest singer', until, like a true rebel, he rebelled against that label. For if Dylan was interested in anything other than making music and manufacturing his own myth, his bent lay more in poetry than in politics. In his spare time, he tinkered with a tortured poetic novel named *Tarantula*.

Then he composed 'Like A Rolling Stone', which rewrote the rule book of rock music. Rich in imagery and word music, it was about twice the length of the average pop song of the time, and demonstrated, not least to Dylan himself, that the possibilities of the form were far wider than had been generally assumed. It was the start of an incredibly fertile few years for the singer, when his brilliant albums came down like snow. Yet by the end of the 1960s, exhausted and ravaged by drug abuse, he felt his muse had abandoned him.

The backlash began. Critics cut and slashed at his lack-lustre releases, until finally, as Dylan himself put it, he worked out how to do consciously what he had once been able to do without effort. The result was 1975's *Blood on the Tracks*, a serious contender for the title of the greatest album ever. The 1980s proved a leaner decade for the singer. Yet since then he has kept coming back. There are even diehard fans who rate his more recent albums as highly as his earliest. This is despite the fact that what there was of his voice has long since gone. The buzz saw is broken, the harmonica battered, but people still believe that he's telling the truth.

Vivienne Westwood, fashion designer (b. 1941)

'My aim is to make the poor look rich and the rich look poor,' the British fashion designer Vivienne Westwood once declared. This remark, which displays her notable quotability, reveals what has been the persistent theme of her career: her love-hate relationship with the establishment. Born into a working-class family in Derbyshire, she moved to London when she was seventeen and worked as a primary school teacher. Although she never received formal training, Westwood was always fascinated by clothes. She made her own wedding dress when, at the age of 21, she married her first husband, Derek. That union came to an end after she met and fell in love with a young impresario and troublemaker named Malcolm McLaren.

In 1971 the couple opened a fashion boutique in the King's Road, which was at first called Let It Rock, and later Sex, Too Fast To Live Too Young To Die, and Seditionaries: a handy summary of some of cool's recurring motifs, which was presumably the point. McLaren and Westwood were button-pushers who launched the punk movement. A musical style, a way of dressing and an attitude to life, it was devoted to a single aim, which was to get a reaction out of the

stuffed shirts. What would most disgust them? An emphasis on the seedy side of things, so Westwood put her skills
to work designing punk clothing out of leather and rubber,
inspired by bondage gear. What would most offend them?
An attack, perhaps, on the royal family. Accordingly, in the
week of the Silver Jubilee, the punk band The Sex Pistols,
helmed by John Lydon and managed by McLaren, released
the sneering, anti-monarchist anthem 'God Save the Queen'.
Westwood has claimed she personally came up with the title
of, and idea behind, their best-known single, 'Anarchy in the
UK' (although Lydon has dismissed this as 'audacity of the
highest order').

After she and McLaren split acrimoniously (he was 'not',
she has observed mildly, 'a very nice man') Westwood went
on to take the best conceivable revenge by being much more
successful than him. The fashion label they founded together
became hers alone, and courted international attention by
playing with stereotypical ideas of Britishness. 'It's not possible to produce anything exotic except through something
traditional,' she has said, when asked about her fascination
with such old-school fabrics as tweed and tartan.

Muhammad Ali, boxer (1942—2016)

Muhammad Ali stands over boxing like a colossus. He
achieved that status not so much by being the best boxer of
all time (although you could make that argument). It was by
being more than a boxer. He was handsome, an accomplished

clown, a clever speaker whose pre-match recitals – either bigging himself up or doing down his opponents – were a stylistic precursor to the verbal preening of hip hop. 'I have wrestled with an alligator,' he declared in 1974. 'I done tussled with a whale. I done handcuffed lightning. Thrown thunder in jail. Only last week, I murdered a rock. Injured a stone. Hospitalised a brick. I'm so mean, I make medicine sick.'

This was in the run-up to the so-called 'Rumble in the Jungle', his battle with George Foreman, which took place in the sweltering heat of Zaire. By then, Ali was a venerable 32, while Foreman, the heavyweight title-holder, was a youthful 25 and reputed to be the hardest hitter in the history of the sport. There were fears Ali would literally be killed. It seemed a mythic encounter, and, like a character from myth, the weaker man deployed brains against brawn. Ali had always been known for the lightning speed of his feet, which enabled him to evade brutal antagonists such as Sonny Liston and Joe Frazier. But to his fans' dismay, against Foreman he leaned back against the ropes, covered his face with his gloves, and let the big man hit him. This Foreman did, unleashing a tirade of hammer blows, but failing to cause serious damage. From time to time, Ali would goad him, asking, 'Is that the best you can do, George?' Eventually Foreman tired, and Ali came back into the fight, astonishing the world by knocking his opponent out in the eighth round.

A great man, but not a perfect one, Ali succumbed to the temptations of fame and had a string of extra-marital affairs. He also joined the black-rights group the Nation of

Islam, notwithstanding the fact that some of their beliefs were frankly potty. (Their founder asserted that the white race was created by a mad scientist in a deranged eugenics experiment on the Greek island of Patmos.) Yet it was Ali's adherence to their creed that led him to refuse to fight in Vietnam in 1967. As a result, he became the most hated man in America. He was stripped of his titles and banned from fighting for three years in the prime of his career. However, as the tide of feeling slowly turned against the war, people began to whisper that perhaps Ali had been right all along. Paradoxically, he found himself a countercultural hero: the pugilist who wouldn't fight.

Jimi Hendrix, musician (1942–70)

Rock music has been the white man's answer to the blues. The black man's answer to rock music is Jimi Hendrix. In a white-dominated genre, the Seattle-born guitarist is a rare example of a black star – one for whom the generally white and middle-class (not to say middle-aged) critics tend to sprint through their store of superlatives. The greatest rock guitarist of all time? Check. The greatest instrumentalist in the history of rock music? Hang on a second: doesn't the first of those automatically entail the second? All of which makes it rather difficult to assess Hendrix's impact and influence with an unjaundiced eye.

Watching footage of his live performances at the end of the 1960s, you're struck by how crassly sexual much of it is (with moments, for instance, when Hendrix flickers his tongue suggestively at his female fans) and by the circus tricks: the times he plays his guitar with his teeth, for example, or behind his back. Which might leave anyone over the age of sixteen thinking: so what? Clearly, the man was a virtuoso instrumentalist, who wielded his Fender Stratocaster guitar like a wizard or countercultural shaman (and who dressed to match, favouring broad-brimmed hats, snaky jeans and Carnaby Street furs). But how much of his unassailable status in the iconography of rock is down to publicity stunts, such as when he set his guitar on fire on stage at Monterey in 1967, and to his tragically early death at the age of 27 from a drugs overdose?

Then you turn to the music. Numbers such as 'Voodoo Chile (Slight Return)', which, opening with what sounds like the whirring rotor blades of a helicopter (actually created by Hendrix's guitar), must be one the greatest rock songs of all time. Ditto his cover of Bob Dylan's* 'All Along the Watchtower'. The size of the sound, wrapped in feedback and vibrating to his innovative use of the wah-wah pedal, may strike some as overpowering, as may the heady, heavy, hallucinogenic vibe. But he could do softer, as in the shimmering 'May This Be Love'. And in person he seems to have been a gentle soul, except when he touched hard liquor. It should be noted too that Hendrix is revered as much by musicians as he is by critics. Eric Clapton said his life was changed by hearing him play. And Dylan, writing about Hendrix's version of 'All Along the Watchtower', expressed disappointment that he hadn't covered more of his songs. After all, he said, 'they're all his'.

Lou Reed, singer and songwriter (1942–2013)

The Velvet Underground, of which Lou Reed was lead singer, was the most successful unsuccessful band of all time. As the music producer Brian Eno once put it, few people bought their 1967 debut LP, but everyone who did went on to form a band of their own. One of the most striking things about their music, and about Reed's later solo stuff, was how little they seemed to care about whether anyone cared. The song 'Heroin' describes how it feels to shoot up: a rush and come-down that the song recreates sonically. The oppressive, depressive 'Venus in Furs' was inspired by the S&M novel of the same name by Leopold von Sacher-Masoch. Clearly, this was not a band courting the mainstream.

The son of a Brooklyn accountant, Reed was subjected to brutal electroconvulsive therapy as a teenager, with the aim of 'curing' him of his homosexual tendencies. The treatment sealed his anger towards the establishment. On stage with the Velvets, in his black leather jacket, his face emotionless behind his aviator shades, as he forced a barrage of distorted noise from his guitar, he seemed an avenging angel subjecting the world to his own form of electroconvulsive therapy. He was never an easy guy to get along with. After the band split up in 1970, Reed vanished off the radar for a couple of years. It later transpired he had been working for his dad.

When he returned to New York to launch a solo career, he enjoyed the biggest hit of his career with the single 'Walk on the Wild Side', a hummable lullaby, complete with sax solo, which was actually about gay prostitution. As ever, it featured hip, poetic lyrics and Reed's trademark New York drawl, more of a speaking than a singing voice, as if he couldn't be bothered to break into fully-fledged song.

Supported by the patronage of Andy Warhol* (who designed the artwork for their first album), the Velvets built a bridge between the art world and the avant-garde music scene. They wore shades, dressed in black, performed songs about drugs and transgressive sex, and rarely cracked a smile. And they were beyond good. The coolest band in history? Quite possibly. And how about Reed himself? By all accounts, he was aggressive in person, nursing particular resentment towards interviewers, especially of the English variety. The definition of 'misery', he once said, was 'being interviewed by an English journalist'. In later life, he cleaned up and settled down with his third wife, Laurie Anderson, practising tai chi to relieve his feelings.

Janis Joplin, singer (1943–70)

The crazy, dazed, drug-taking, heartbreaking rock 'n' roll singer Janis Joplin sometimes seems like an embodiment of the counterculture in all of its good qualities as well as some of its bad. By her own account, she just wanted to be loved. But after finding that this didn't come to her conventionally, she jettisoned her home state of Texas, and travelled to San Francisco to became a rock star.

Joplin wasn't beautiful. At high school, she had been crassly voted the 'ugliest man on campus' by her contemporaries. But when she opened her mouth to sing, the sound that came out was remarkable: a wrenched soul singer's voice of great pain and power, out of control at times, but with an unignorable force. This made her sexy, all the more so, perhaps, for the mortal plainness of her features. She had affairs with the talk show host Dick Cavett* and fellow singer Kris Kristofferson (who gifted her her biggest hit, letting her cover his song 'Me and Bobby McGee'). It was when she was singing that she felt most desirable, she said, but it was a temporary fix. 'On stage, I make love to 25,000 people, then I go home alone,' she once declared plaintively. Revealingly, her definition of 'ambition' was 'the desire for love', which in her case was so great it may have been impossible to satisfy. When there was no one around for a fling, Joplin medicated her loneliness with booze and hard drugs.

Having always been told that she was different, she resolved to look the part, sporting hippyish granny glasses, ethnic clothes, and beads and feathers in her unkempt hair. It was part of her determination to be extraordinary, no matter what the cost. 'Man, I'd rather have ten years of super-hyper-most,' she insisted, 'than live to be 70 by sitting in some goddamn chair watching TV.' In the event, she died of a heroin* overdose at the age of 27, just a fortnight after Jimi Hendrix* had met the same fate.

Keith Richards, musician (b. 1943)

Keith Richards has the reputation of being perhaps the coolest man alive. Partly this is down to his virtuosity as lead guitarist of the Rolling Stones, and as one half, along with the singer Mick Jagger, of a writing partnership that has produced a scorching repertoire of classic rock songs including 'Honky Tonk Women' and 'Jumpin' Jack Flash'. But Richards' cool status arguably owes more to two less artistic feats. First, it's the way that, while wielding his guitar behind an extraordinarily charismatic frontman, he has often looked wryly unimpressed. In other words, he may not be able to dance like Jagger, but he has always acted cooler. Second, he's revered for having taken a phenomenal amount of drugs without actually expiring, even if the result has been that he increasingly resembles an elderly lizard which has been repeatedly struck by lightning, despite the advice of friends that it might be time to come in out of the rain.

With an air somewhere between bewildered and piratical*, the guitarist has been described by the louche music critic Nick Kent as being, like Lord Byron*, 'mad, bad and dangerous to know'. Yet the most striking revelation of his excellent autobiography is what a thoroughly decent cove Richards clearly is. The book also confirms something we had long suspected, that high among his gifts has been the possession of a cast-iron bullshit detector. Hence his arched eyebrow at Jagger's preening and prancing.

Of course, he has had other reasons for scepticism towards his band mate, not least among them the suspicion that Jagger was sleeping with his girlfriend, Anita Pallenberg*, while the two of them were acting together in *Performance* back in 1968. Meanwhile, hunkered down in digs belonging to his friend Robert Fraser*, Richards channelled his ominous, oppressed mood to compose 'Gimme Shelter'. With its bruised, brooding tone, the song has been interpreted as an anthem calling attention to the tawdry end of the 1960s dream. Maybe so. But thanks to Richards' autobiography we now know that it is also, on some level, the song of a man who fears that his best friend may be banging his girl. Richards being Richards, he didn't bear a grudge, or not much of a one.

'We are not old men. We are not worried about petty morals,' the guitarist famously declared during the trial that followed the Stones' infamous drugs bust in 1967. Now, of course, he *is* an old man. But, in the context of his past, one among Richards' many achievements has been to make his visible agedness a badge of honour.

Anita Pallenberg, actress (1944–2017)

What can you say about a woman who was once regarded as being a 'bad influence' on Keith Richards*? The model, muse and femme fatale Anita Pallenberg met the Rolling Stones at a concert in Munich in 1965. She went out with the troubled band member Brian Jones, who frequently came off worse in their physical fights. Later she transferred her affections to Richards. She 'scared the pants off me', the latter once confessed, much to the satisfaction of Pallenberg, who, on hearing of the comment long afterwards, observed, 'I still do.' But her influence went deeper than that. Mick Jagger took her opinions seriously enough that, after her critique, he rewrote several songs on the band's classic album *Beggars Banquet*.

A long-limbed blonde German–Italian beauty, Pallenberg devoted her early years to living it up in style. As a teen-ager, she hung out in Rome with the likes of the film-maker Federico Fellini and the novelist Alberto Moravia. A few years later, she popped up in New York, where she befriended Andy Warhol* and the Beat poets. Although she never achieved serious acclaim as an actress, she starred in two of the iconic movies of the era. In the high-camp sci-fi *Barbarella* (1968) she played the villainous Great Tyrant, while in 1970's *Performance* she was one of the two group-ies who romp in bed with Mick Jagger's decadent pop star. According to Keith Richards' bodyguard Tony Sanchez, she seduced Jagger during filming, and took enormous pleasure in having gone to bed with yet another Rolling Stone. But the account of Sanchez, who appears to have had an axe to grind, may not be reliable. He also recalled that Pallenberg was 'obsessed with black magic* and began to carry a string of garlic with her everywhere – even to bed – to ward off vampires*'.

During the 1970s, around the same time as they became unmarried parents, she and Richards also got hooked on her-oin*. Their lives spiralled out of control, and they eventually separated. In 1979, Pallenberg's seventeen-year-old lover shot himself at her New York apartment. She finally managed to break her drug and booze dependency, and ended up leading a relatively sedate life in London, attending Alcoholics Anonymous and visiting her allotment in Chiswick. The model Kate Moss*, one of her closest friends, has described her as 'a big influence'.

Marianne Faithfull, actress and singer (b. 1946)

Marianne Faithfull and Anita Pallenberg* sometimes seem like reverse sides of the same coin. Former girlfriends of the Rolling Stones, they were both also singers and actors, frustrated at finding themselves sidelined while their other halves got on with the 'men's work' of being in one of the world's biggest rock bands. But while Pallenberg is remembered for the pain she inflicted as a femme fatale, Faithfull has been cast as a sacrificial victim, defined by what she has suffered, and survived, albeit by the skin of her teeth.

In this context, it seems fitting that Faithfull is related via her Austrian mother to the novelist Leopold von Sacher-Masoch (from whom we get the word 'masochist'). She was first spotted at the age of seventeen at a party by the Stones' manager, Andrew Loog Oldham, who later described her as 'an angel with big tits'. Sensing she had star quality, he instructed Mick Jagger and Keith Richards* to write a song for her. They came up with 'As Tears Go By', which Faithfull took to the top of the charts. From 1966 to 1970, she went out with Jagger. It was she who introduced him to the Bulgakov novel *The Master and Margarita*, thereby inspiring him to write the classic Stones number 'Sympathy for the Devil', on which Pallenberg sang backing vocals. While Pallenberg and Jagger cavorted on the set of *Performance* in 1968, Faithfull and Richards consoled themselves with a fling of their own. Both Pallenberg and Faithfull would also become junkies, though addiction hit Faithfull harder and sooner.

Her talent provided consolation. Despite being reduced, at her lowest point in the 1970s, to living on the streets of Soho, she was repeatedly able to make a career comeback, and although her music now seems something of a footnote to the Stones' back catalogue, in her day albums such as *Broken English* (1979), which features the haunting 'Ballad of Lucy Jordan', enjoyed considerable success. She has also achieved acclaim as an actress, whose filmography includes an early turn as Ophelia in a production of *Hamlet** opposite the mercurial Nicol Williamson. One of rock music's great survivors, she appeared more recently in Sofia Coppola's* *Marie-Antoinette*. She played the heroine's mother, bringing to the role her still-striking looks, a cracked, ex-addict's voice, and the air of one who had achieved wisdom, as the Greeks used to recommend, through suffering.

Patti Smith, singer and poet (b. 1946)

To anyone who has any desire to argue that women aren't as cool as men, the punk poet Patti Smith provides a powerful response. The image of her on the cover of her debut album *Horses* (1975) is a masterclass in attitude. She stands like a street dandy, her style combining an old-fashioned aesthetic (the braces and the pinstripes) with a shabby modernity (the mop of hair and the coat slung over one shoulder). In her head's tilt, and the slenderness of her neck and wrists, the stance simultaneously suggests a defiance and sensitivity that can also be heard in the songs. 'Gloria', the opening number on *Horses*, kicks off with Smith sneeringly intoning that Jesus died for somebody's sins, but not hers. It's a rejection of organised religion, but also a complex, cultured enough idea to represent a rejection of crass rock simplicity.

Throughout her career, Smith has displayed a knack for having her cake and eating it. 'Gloria' sounded completely fresh, but was, of course, a cover version (of Van Morrison's original). An acclaimed poet, she enjoyed her biggest hit with 1978's 'Because the Night', which was actually written by Bruce Springsteen. After achieving considerable success as a female rock star in a male-dominated industry, she ducked out of the limelight, leaving New York and moving to Michigan to focus on bringing up her children. She released only one album over the next seventeen years. What renders this so magnificently cool is the way that, this being done, she casually picked up her career where she had left it. In other words, when it suited her to be a rock star, she was; when not, not. She does what she wants, when she wants.

It's a hard call, but the coolest Patti Smith song is probably the nine-minute epic 'Birdland' off her first album. However, Kurt Cobain's* widow Courtney Love once said that 1978's 'Rock 'n' Roll Nigger' is not only Smith's greatest song, but the greatest rock song of all time. On it she declared that Jimi Hendrix*, Jesus Christ and Jackson Pollock* were all 'niggers', before intoning 'nigger, nigger, nigger' defiantly. There are a lot of observations one could make about these lyrics. But one of them is that they show that the author is a student of cool, who knows her subject.

David Bowie, singer and songwriter (1947–2016)

David Bowie didn't invent reinvention, but he was the first rock star to make it his calling card. The question, at least in the 1970s, wasn't what he would do next, but who he would be. First came Ziggy Stardust, the glam-rock alien; then there was the androgynous superstar Aladdin Sane, his face split by a dark birthmark of lightning; and later the Thin White Duke, a haughty, angst-ridden aristocratic type who seemed to be a personification of the cocaine addiction that by then blighted the singer's life. In each case, the fact that he gave the character a name made the same, modishly postmodernist* point: it wasn't him. And each new look was also accompanied by a new style of music, ranging from rock 'n' roll and music-hall to soul, reggae, rock and jazz.

Throughout his career – with the possible exception of a phase of drug-induced paranoia that almost wrecked him in the late 1970s – Bowie seemed to know exactly what he was doing. You could call him an opportunist: his breakthrough single, 'Space Oddity', was released in the week of the first Moon landing. You could accuse him of jumping on a cool bandwagon: he pretended to be bisexual when (let's be honest about it) he was obviously straight. Early song titles confessed his debt to Bob Dylan* and Andy Warhol*. He claimed to employ a 'cut-up' approach to songwriting, inspired by the Beat novelist William S. Burroughs*. This last, though, was surely a façade or fad. If there was one thing Bowie's lyrics weren't, it was random. On the contrary, they were poetic, provocative and highly articulate, making him Britain's most obvious rival to Bob Dylan for the title of rock's Poet Laureate.

Another thing he had in common with Dylan: whatever the guise, he was always given away by his voice, which was deep, constrained and unmistakable. Nor could Bowie mask his extraordinary features. A thin face. Martini-glass cheek bones. Teeth that were frankly terrifying (barely less so after he got them fixed). And as if that wasn't enough, a boyhood fight had damaged his left eye, making it, in certain lights, look a different colour to his right. Even without the make-up, Bowie moved among men like a being from another world.

Richard Branson, businessman (b. 1950)

Apple's 1997 'Think Different' ad presented a list of inspiring mavericks who had shaped the 20th century. There was Bob Dylan* and Muhammad Ali*. There was Martin Luther King and Mohandas Gandhi. There was (hang on a second) Richard Branson? You'd be forgiven for wondering how the bearded, grinning, British ex-public-school entrepreneur, most readily pictured waving from a hot-air balloon, merited inclusion. The answer is that he's a philanthropist (recently devoted to the cause of saving the planet from environmental cataclysm). He's also one of the most obvious examples (the beard is a give-away) of a businessman steeped in the 1960s values among which he grew up. All of which is a roundabout way of saying that Branson is cool.

Wait. Hold up again. Really? Who are we kidding? In person Branson seems like an overexcited yellow Labrador. Nervous, keen to please, but basically a geek, albeit an endearing and even quite an attractive one. The real reason for his appearance in that ad alongside such titans is that he's a stand-in for the Apple CEO Steve Jobs*, with whom he had a lot in common. Both geeks*, familiar with the paraphernalia of coolness, they realised cool could be used to sell not only jeans and T-shirts, but anything. Both won over a fanbase by appealing directly to the emotions via music: Jobs came up with the iPod; in Branson's case, it was his Virgin Records label, Virgin Megastores and even Virgin FM (which was devoted to playing music by the likes of Bob Dylan). Then when they moved on respectively to selling mobile phones (the iPhone) and transatlantic flights (with Virgin Atlantic), their customers came too.

Branson's method is to find an industry dominated by a corporate giant and present his company as the cool alternative. (His airline squared up to British Airways, for instance, and gave it a bloody nose.) He himself accepts the David and Goliath analogy, once remarking that 'It's a hell of a lot more fun being in the David role.' The problem with this approach is that if it succeeds, it fails. Which is to say that if the underdog beats the favourite, it becomes the favourite; if the outsider takes down the insider, he ceases to be an outsider. That's the way it has been with Branson, as it was with Jobs. This doesn't mean they make less money. But perhaps it makes them less cool. Or if not, it devalues, a little, the meaning of the word.

DJ Kool Herc, DJ (b. 1955)

In the early 1970s, a Jamaican kid named Clive threw a party at his home in the Bronx. He had noticed that the point when the dance floor usually went crazy was the instrumental 'break' that came towards the end of a song. To extend it, he set up copies of the same disc on two turntables. When the first reached the end of the break he switched to the second, which then played the break again. This technique, which soon caught on, made space for the development of a flashy style of solo dancing that became known as 'break-dancing'. It is one of the four component parts of hip hop culture, along with graffiti art, DJ-ing and rapping, in all of which Clive, better known to fans and friends as DJ Kool Herc, had a hand.

Born in Kingston, he moved to New York with his parents when he was twelve. In his teens, he joined a graffiti crew called the Ex-Vandals, yet he was always more interested in being a DJ than in the gang rivalry that then plagued the Bronx. Because of his heroically muscular build, which was particularly evident when he played basketball, he earned the nickname DJ Kool Herc (Herc being short for Hercules). From doubling the length of the break, Herc went on to treble and quadruple it, creating what he called the 'merry-go-round' during which the break-dancers, whom he dubbed 'b-boys' and 'b-girls', did their thing. There was also increased opportunity for DJs to encourage the dancers by 'toasting' them over the mike, which Herc did with rhyming patter. 'This is the joint! Herc beat on the point!' he might shout, for example; or alternatively, 'B-boys, b-girls, are you ready? Keep on, rock steady!'

DJ Kool Herc became a local hero in his part of the Bronx and is now regarded as first among equals of the triumvirate credited with inventing hip hop. Unlike the other two, Afrika Bambaataa and Grandmaster Flash, he never made money out of it. This may explain why he retains an aura of particular integrity. For Herc, it was only ever about the party.

Steve Jobs, businessman (1955–2011)

'Here's to the crazy ones,' the TV ad began. 'The misfits. The rebels. The troublemakers. The round pegs in the square holes.' You'd be forgiven for thinking this was a trailer for a documentary* about the rise of cool, especially since the voice-over spiel accompanied footage of characters who might be thought to embody that quality, including Bob Dylan*, Richard Branson*, John Lennon*, Muhammad Ali* and Amelia Earhart*. But as a matter of fact, it was a commercial promoting Apple computers, inspired and endorsed in 1997 by the company's controversial co-founder and CEO, Steve Jobs. He didn't write the text (which was a variation on a famous paean in praise of 'the mad ones' in Jack Kerouac's* *On the Road*), but it neatly summed up his maverick self-image. It went without saying that the final figure missing from the ad was Jobs himself.

The trouble with this eccentric, extraordinary figure is that on a personal level, he was reputed to be a bit of a git: rude, controlling, and with a rampant Messiah complex of which he wasn't ashamed. (He once attended a party dressed as Jesus Christ.) At Apple headquarters, employees used to dread finding themselves trapped in a lift with him, for fear that he might fire them on a whim. For a long time he denied paternity of his daughter Lisa, and even after that was proven by a DNA test, he only grudgingly paid child support, despite being phenomenally rich. The man was also a geek*. His constant attire – Levi 501s and a black turtleneck sweater – was a uniform of sorts, so he didn't have to think about what to wear. Yet in Jobs's lifetime, a revolutionary notion arose, partly motivated by his own example: that geekdom and coolness were compatible.

In a world transformed by mobile phones, computers and the internet, the man who provided the gadgets was the transforming agent. There was more, though, to Jobs's achievement than launching such iconic products as the iPod, the iPhone and Mac computers. He personally tailored his Apple brand, favouring a blend of simplicity and sleekness over all else. His masterstroke was to link this look with a cool life philosophy of personal fulfilment. 'Don't settle,' he would advise his fans at the ecstatic launches for his beloved products. 'Stay hungry. Find what you love.'

Madonna, singer (b. 1958)

The fact that Madonna is the most successful female solo artist of all time is curious. She doesn't have an amazing voice. When she first moved to New York aged nineteen – with only $35 in her pocket, so the story goes – her aim was to make it as a dancer. But she isn't an extraordinary dancer. Nor is she unusually beautiful, though she has a great figure, which she maintains with impressive discipline. Even her songs haven't been so terrific, with the exceptions of 'Vogue', and 'Like a Prayer', which begins with the observation that life is a mystery. Madonna's career, then, might be described as a fact of life.

Maybe you don't need to excel in any one area if you have her range of skills. That full house – a good-looking performer, with a decent voice, who can also dance – is rarer than one might think. And you have to add to it the fact that she has always had an instinctive understanding of what people want. A businesswoman first, then, and an entertainer second. In the oddly engrossing (albeit in places staggeringly banal) fly-on-the-wall documentary* *Madonna: Truth or Dare*, she allows the cameras to follow her practically everywhere as she embarks on her Blond Ambition tour of 1990. We see her simulate masturbation on stage, chat with her disconcerted father after the show, snub an old friend, and laugh and flirt with her visibly nervous backing dancers. The only time she demands privacy is when she needs to discuss money. 'Get out!' she tells the film-makers firmly. 'I'm having a business talk. Goodbye!'

The intensity of her blond ambition is itself pretty revolutionary. Madonna isn't someone who apologises for knowing what she wants. In person, she seems like a hard-faced Marilyn Monroe who happens to be in control of her destiny. This is one of the reasons why women love her. Because the message of her success is that you can be sexy *and* kick ass. Another secret ingredient is that she's utterly childlike. Any claim that her raunchy stage shows are 'exploring themes of sexuality' is laughable. Throughout her career, her treatment of sexual themes has been about as profound as that of a schoolgirl flashing her knickers in the back of the class. For a lot of people, this is evidently what they want. Whatever else you want to say about it, it's fun.

Quentin Tarantino, film-maker (b. 1963)

Watching a movie by Quentin Tarantino, you can almost hear his voice saying, 'Now *this* is cool.' These are the coolest actors. These are the coolest songs. These are the coolest scenarios and coolest pay-off lines that he, or anyone else, can write. In *Pulp Fiction* (1994), Bruce Willis is taken prisoner by two sadistic fetishists, one of whom is called Zed. He manages to break free, kills one of them, and then roars off on a Harley Davidson, after explaining to his bewildered girlfriend, 'Zed's dead, baby. Zed's dead.' Why does he repeat the line? Because it sounds cool.

It's hard to think of a film-maker more devoted to cool as a value above all others. That very narrowness, you might say, comes close to being uncool of him. And it may partly explain why there has been a dip in the quality of his output after the thunder and lightning of his arrival on the scene. This isn't to say that his more recent films, such as *The Hateful Eight*, are bad, exactly. They just can't compete with the coolness of his first, *Reservoir Dogs*, a violent bank-heist thriller with a script as slick as a David Mamet play, or his second, **Pulp Fiction*, which is possibly the coolest film ever made by anyone. You have to acknowledge that Tarantino added new qualities to the dog-eared concept of cool. Notably his super-smart dialogue, in which bad guys bicker like children, or a Madonna* song is subjected to wry pseudo-intellectual scrutiny. Also a trendily postmodern* non-linear approach to storytelling, favouring multiple narratives and zigzagging timelines. But otherwise the most striking Tarantino-esque quality is nostalgia. He has favoured films set in, or rich in the ethos of, or inspired by genres created during, the 1960s and 1970s.

When he was a twenty-something nobody, Tarantino worked in an LA video store. In the process, he acquired a vast cinematic knowledge, which his movies display with self-conscious homages. Before he was anyone, Tarantino was a geek*, and, rather endearingly, he still is. The trouble is that, while in his first films the fanboy expertise fed his originality, since then his works have been variations on a stylistic theme. They seem like exercises, not artworks. There has been a quality of silliness that had previously been kept in check. (Titles such as *Kill Bill* and *Inglourious Basterds* give a sense of the cartoonish streak.) All told, though, his early achievements bestow on him a kind of artistic immunity. It doesn't really matter if he now does this, because he once did that.

Björk, singer and songwriter (b. 1965)

Was 1993 really an incredible year for music, or was it just that I was seventeen and had only just started paying attention? Amid the first stirrings of what was to become Britpop, an album came out that sounded utterly unlike anything else available at the time. Björk's *Debut* betrayed eclectic influences that ranged from electro to Indian, but above all it was her voice that grabbed the attention: the flimsy, childlike breathiness alternating with an almost operatic power, the scat-influenced glottal grunts and exuberant yells (that rodeo cry of 'yee-hah!' on 'Big Time Sensuality', for instance), and her pretty, precious-sounding Icelandic accent, with a hint of cockney, as she ran her tongue over the absurdities of the English language.

Despite the album's title, and although she was not yet thirty, Björk Guðmundsdóttir had already enjoyed success as lead singer of the Icelandic art-rock group The Sugarcubes. Since then, her releases have often been obscure, rarely easy, yet somehow she has stayed mainstream. The key to that paradox owes something to her pixie dream-girl looks and eccentricities. When she attacked a photographer who'd been hassling her in Bangkok airport, it seemed in keeping with her child-of-nature persona. Lars von Trier channelled this in his film *Dancer in the Dark*, in which Björk's turn as a woman struggling to pay for an operation to prevent her son going blind earned her the Best Actress Award at the 2000 Cannes Film Festival. When she appeared at the Oscars wearing a dress that looked like a swan was draped around her neck, it met with derision. It has since been voted one of the most iconic red carpet outfits of all time.

'Feminists bore me to death,' Björk once declared. 'I follow my instinct and if that supports young girls in any way, great. But I'd rather they saw it more as a lesson about following their own instincts.' Her statements can seem studied. When she claimed that her greatest musical influence was the broadcaster David Attenborough, it may have been a joke, but it was a nice soundbite all the same. Yet she could get away with it, thanks to her air of insouciance, her perennial popularity, and, above all, her extraordinary vocal talents.

Kurt Cobain, singer and songwriter (1967–94)

The rock singer Kurt Cobain was a classic case of the boy who never grew up. Before killing himself with a shotgun at the age of 27 he wrote a suicide note, observing that it was 'better to burn out than fade away' (a quote from a Neil Young song). The note was addressed not to his wife or daughter, but to his imaginary childhood friend, Boddha. The most successful album by his 1990s rock group Nirvana was called *Nevermind*. The title was not only a characteristic expression of adolescent indifference (cf. the Miles Davis number 'So What?') but also an allusion to Neverland, the mythical place where Peter Pan enjoyed his unending youth.

The fixative trauma of Cobain's childhood growing up in Seattle had been his parents' divorce, which left him feeling rejected, a loner who empathised with underdogs. (One of his teenage diary entries declared, 'I am not gay, although I wish I were, just to piss off homophobes.') Tragically, the association with society's outsiders made his success with Nirvana, and elevation to spokesman for his generation, impossible to process. Yet *Nevermind* was so good, it could hardly have failed to attract attention. Songs such as 'Lithium' and 'Smells like Teen Spirit' swung with deliberate bipolarity between a soft/indie and a hard/metal sound, and the result-ing style, which was dubbed 'grunge', offered something for everyone. The latter song's title was in part a jokey reference to a popular female deodorant of the time called Teen Spirit, but also it was a mocking allusion to the schoolboy notion of 'team spirit': the kind of social ideal against which Cobain consciously aligned himself.

When, days after his death, his wife Courtney Love read out excerpts from his suicide note to devastated fans, she called the singer an 'asshole' for killing himself. Did she have a point? This was a guy who was rich, handsome and talented. But read his note, in which he refers to himself as a 'death rocker' and 'sad little, sensitive, unappreciative, Pisces, Jesus man', and it seems an inappropriate response. Lest we forget, Cobain was also a heroin* addict who suffered agony from an undiagnosed stomach condition. Some fans believe he was murdered: his note, they say, was forged, or it wasn't a suicide note. This is straw-clutching. His music too, particularly on the band's final album *In Utero*, is soaked in self-disgust and misery. The mystery is how it's possible for anyone to enjoy it. Perhaps, as Aristotle suggested about Greek tragedy, it's the cathartic release or relief of experiencing an unhappiness that so comprehensively out-fathoms your own.

Sofia Coppola, film-maker (b. 1971)

After watching a James Bond* film, men tend to walk out of the cinema ahead of their girlfriends. After Sofia Coppola's 2003 movie *Lost in Translation*, the reverse was true. Women strode out ahead of their male companions, feeling empowered by a rare example of an intelligent film that spoke to them directly. The bittersweet comedy, set in a Tokyo hotel, deals with the romantic friendship between two of the guests: an ageing movie star (Bill Murray) and a winsome, wistful twenty-something (Scarlett Johansson) who has doubts about her marriage to a vain young photographer. That word 'friendship' is key. Murray and Johansson don't sleep together (not least because they are both married). In our era of instant gratification, this seemed revolutionary.

Rebelling intelligently against the prevailing value system

is at the heart of what it means to be cool. Murray's character does it and so does Johansson's (one of the reasons they feel drawn to each other). Above all, though, it's what the film itself does. *Lost in Translation* takes the age gap between its leads to an extreme, daring to dramatise the kind of Electra complex that is far more common in reality than is often admitted by Hollywood. It's also an example of what is sometimes termed a 'post-romance film', meaning that it questions the 20th-century obsession with love, and suggests there may, just possibly, be more to life than committed monogamy.

Then there's the ending. On his way to the airport, after bidding Johansson a stilted goodbye, Murray spots her in the bustling Tokyo streets. He stops his taxi. The two hug and he whispers something in her ear, which the audience don't get to hear. Films are founded on the notion of being able to eavesdrop on the significant emotional exchanges of their characters. Yet here was one that seemed to say: some things are too private to be shared, even in a movie.

The story goes that Murray improvised the moment. But the film is above all the achievement of its director, who also wrote the script. It earned Coppola a Best Original Screenplay Oscar when she was just 32, an achievement that was arguably not less impressive, but more so, for the fact that her father is Francis Ford Coppola, one of the greatest directors in Hollywood history. She has stepped out from his shadow to create a serious body of work characterised by its distinctive style, intelligence and some terrific 1980s-style soundtracks.

Biggie Smalls, singer and songwriter (1972–97)

Christopher Wallace, professionally known as Biggie Smalls, The Notorious B.I.G., or simply Biggie, described himself on one of his songs as 'black and ugly'. He certainly wasn't conventionally beautiful. Like a black Socrates*, he was over-weight, with a snub nose and dark, lazy-lidded eyes. But his inspired 'flow' at the mike – that's to say, his facility and felicity with words – earned him a global reputation, which was sealed by his murder at the age of 24. He is widely regarded as one of the greatest rap singers of all time.

He didn't write down the lyrics to his songs. He would work them out in his head in the studio, nodding to himself, lips moving silently. Then he would deliver them to perfection, in his throaty, slightly adenoidal voice. Owing to his early death, he only had time to complete two albums, whose morbid titles (*Ready To Die* and *Life After Death*) retrospectively seemed to prefigure his fate. Fans make high claims for the ground-breaking nature of the themes. His song *Juicy*, for instance, which contrasts his new-found wealth and success with his origins as a poor kid growing up on the streets of Brooklyn, has been hailed as a manifesto of social mobility. Equally, some say his songs about relationships explore complex emotional themes, although titles such as 'Me And My Bitch' may suggest otherwise. On 'Want the Old Thing Back', Biggie boasts that he's guaranteed to 'f***' any woman until she gets a nosebleed.

When Biggie rapped about his criminal past, he wasn't, unlike some, making it up. He had begun selling drugs as a kid and in 1991 served nine months in jail for dealing crack cocaine. There was then a violent rivalry between drug gangs, and rival rapping styles, originating in east- and west-coast America. Bad feeling arose between Biggie and his former friend, the California rapper Tupac Shakur. After the latter was gunned down in 1996, a rumour sprang up that Biggie was linked to the killing. The following year, he was in LA on his way to a party to celebrate the release of his second album, when his SUV paused at traffic lights. A car drew up alongside and shots were fired. Biggie was pronounced dead an hour later.

Kate Moss, model (b. 1974)

On the day of the supermodel Kate Moss's wedding, she confessed to her friend, the fashioner designer John Galliano, that she was freaking out. 'Who am I?' she demanded. 'You've got to give me a character.' Galliano told her that she was the last of the English roses, but that when the groom lifted the veil, he would 'see her wanton past'. In part this was a conventional request from a model, who will often be given a role to play on a shoot. But it's also instructive: not only Galliano's answer, but the fact that Moss felt compelled to ask the question.

One reason she has managed to stay at the top of her profession for a quarter of a century, which is about five times longer than the shelf life of most top models, is that she started so early, being talent-spotted at the age of fourteen.

Another is that – like her, it seems – we're not entirely sure who she is. Although she's more relaxed about it these days, for years she didn't give interviews, adopting Benjamin Disraeli's maxim 'Never complain, never explain.' She was known as the 'anti-supermodel', not because she wasn't beautiful, which of course she was, but because at the same time she looked ordinary. She looked, in other words, like the kind of incredibly beautiful girl you might spot in the street: a fresh canvas onto which you could paint whatever character most appealed to you.

One popular choice has, predictably, been prima donna, but onlookers have also tended to run with wild child, coke fiend and sex maniac (cf. Galliano's reference to her 'wanton past'). That owes something to the company she keeps. A run-through of her exes (who include rockers and bad-boy actors) suggests this might, just possibly, be a girl who likes to party. A kind of confirmation came in 2005 when a tabloid newspaper ran photographs that seemed to show her taking cocaine. Fashion companies cancelled their contracts with Moss and pundits predicted that her career was over. On the contrary, within a year she had bounced back and was earning twice as much as before. Which tends to suggest that her coolness, as manifested in her blend of bohemian rebellion and lightweight mystique, had actually been the secret of her success, all along. Is there a female equivalent of James Dean*, a poster child for the feminine version of cool? In a vote, it's a fair bet Moss would come out on top.

PART TWO:
IDEAS, IDEALS
AND OTHER COOL S***

I tried not to write this book according to any rigid scheme. Most of the subsections that follow map on to one of the Nine Defining Qualities of Cool (see Introduction), but not all of them. As with the Idols list, the approach was to find the subjects that seemed to offer the most insight into what cool is, and then see where that took us.

Fictional idols

Hamlet

The Tragedy of Hamlet, Prince of Denmark (more commonly known as *Hamlet*) wasn't always thought to be the greatest play ever written. For a couple of hundred years, it wasn't even regarded as Shakespeare's best. In the rheumy eyes of aged critics, *King Lear* was more profound. Then, in the era of 19th-century Romanticism, when it became fashionable for brooding poets such as Lord Byron* to flounce around being ostentatiously miserable, *Hamlet*'s stock rose. The youthful protagonist, tortured by an angst he cannot name, seemed to prefigure the Byronic hero. And since the rise of 20th-century cool (which is, at least in part, a democratised version of that Romantic ideal), its status has been practically unassailable.

All of which is preamble for the argument that the personality of Hamlet sketched out several of the definitive qualities of coolness some 350 years before they became cultural currency. Not that to be cool you need to be a member of a Scandinavian royal family, or to have discovered that your father was murdered by your uncle, who then married your mother. But it might help, since if that were your predicament, you might feasibly dress in black, and despise the establishment figures (not least among them your own mother) who carried on as if nothing had happened. You might become obsessed with death, and even conduct a philosophical conversation with a skull, as Hamlet does, finding an external action to express his internal angst.

Nor does this mean that, in order to be cool, you must also be a morbid bore. Hamlet isn't that, necessarily. He's sardonic, it's true, and misanthropic, and he treats his former love Ophelia with neurotic cruelty, wrongly concluding that she's malignly complicit in a conspiracy to manipulate him. But he's also hyper-articulate, highly intelligent, warmly affectionate towards his friends, and often extremely funny. His pretence of madness when he's actually the sanest man around can make for brilliant comedy, while at the same time enacting the classic cool story-type of the apparently hopeless case who emerges as heroic. So it's no surprise to find that Hamlet has loomed large in the minds of some of the primary exponents of cool in the 20th century.

Sarah Bernhardt* and Richard Burton* were both acclaimed for their interpretations of the role. Humphrey Bogart* had mixed feelings about it. He once declared that the only authentic way to award a Best Actor Oscar would be to force every actor to play Hamlet, then make a decision accordingly. However, he also noted, 'I never knew a man who played Hamlet who didn't die broke.' (You can just hear him saying it.) David Bowie*, who nursed thespian ambitions, indulged them in his rock concerts. He had a persona he adopted while touring in 1974, which he called Cracked Actor. Donning sunglasses and a cape, he used to produce a skull and serenade it awhile. Finally, taking morbidity to its natural conclusion, he would plant a kiss on its rictus grin.

Sherlock Holmes

Of the four pillars of what has been conventionally regarded as the good life (home, health, marriage and wealth), the world's most famous fictional detective depends on only one. Sherlock Holmes has a home. He resides in London at 221B Baker Street (although it should be noted that he rents his rooms, as opposed to owning them outright). In all other respects, he is a pioneer of cool, and, as the most portrayed character in movie history, an extremely influential one. The seventy or so actors who have played the great detective include such distinguished and classically trained performers as Basil Rathbone and Benedict Cumberbatch. There have also been less well-known interpretations from the likes of Orson Welles and the James Bond* actor Roger Moore.

Health? Holmes disdains it, fending off boredom by injecting a 7 per cent solution of cocaine, using a syringe he keeps in a Morocco leather case. Marriage? It doesn't appeal. He avoids the opposite sex, noting in one of Arthur Conan Doyle's short stories, which established the character, that women are 'not to be trusted'. Nor, for that matter, does wealth interest him. He has an artistic temperament, relaxing by playing his Stradivarius, assuming he's able to find it amid the bachelor chaos of the digs he shares with his trusty side-kick, Dr Watson. But Holmes's true creativity expresses itself in his superhuman powers of detection. Like a good reader of fiction, he deciphers character and storyline from minute physical details. This is arguably one of the prime reasons for his success and popularity as a fictional character. He's a 'reader', as we are, albeit a preternaturally gifted one. And his gifts inspire us to read better, scouring the prose for clues, and transforming us into temporary detectives.

Holmes benefits, too, from the accompanying attractions of his coolness. Like an ascetic James Bond*, and countless other male-fantasy heroes, he is equal to almost any predicament, including death. After he tumbled to his doom at the Reichenbach Falls in the short story *The Final Problem* (1893), locked in a struggle with his nemesis Professor Moriarty, there was a public outcry. Conan Doyle felt forced to resurrect his Messiah a few years later, in the coolest style imaginable. In *The Adventure of the Empty House*, the detective explains to the astounded Watson that he survived thanks to his handy knowledge of 'baritsu, or the Japanese system of wrestling'. During his absence, he continues, he 'amused himself by visiting Lhassa and spending some days with the head Lama'. He then did a spot of exploring, 'passed through Persia, looked in at Mecca, and paid a short but interesting visit to the Khalifa at Khartoum'. Finally, in a crowning detail, he describes having 'spent some months in research into the coal-tar derivatives'.

James Bond

The history of James Bond has moved in parallel with the history of cool, and either can be used to take the temperature of the other. When Bond thrives, cool is thriving. When film-makers and film-goers forget how to be cool, Bond develops a fever. The books were born about the same time as the birth of classic cool. *Casino Royale*, Ian Fleming's first novel featuring the urbane spy, was published in 1953, the same year as Marlon Brando* appeared in the cinemas in *The Wild One*. The film adaptations reached the screen around the time that cool was entering its maturity in the early 1960s. There was *Dr No* in 1961; *From Russia with Love* in 1963; *Goldfinger* in 1964.

It's not so surprising, therefore, that Bond displays definitive cool characteristics. It goes without saying that he's reckless, a character trait that's exhibited on the large scale when he braves vertiginous heights, ear-shattering explosions and the murderous attentions of psychotic thugs in the name of Queen and country. It exhibits on the small scale too. Heedless of his health, Bond smokes sixty cigarettes a day, favouring a brand with an especially high nicotine content; he drinks heavily; and, in the books, he occasionally takes the amphetamine benzedrine to stay alert, as Jack Kerouac* did while writing *On the Road*. He's also as promiscuous as any Beatnik poet. There's a fine line between emotional coolness and emotional coldness, which 007 crosses repeatedly, as you must if you're going to sleep around with impunity. Admittedly there are the occasional signs that Bond has taken a hit. In the final sentence of *Casino Royale*, after being duped by the beautiful Vesper Lynd, he observes bitterly, 'The bitch is dead now.'

Bond isn't misogynistic, notwithstanding the fact that his boss M describes him as such in the film *Goldeneye*. But he definitely displays qualities of male chauvinism, which were characteristic of the era in which he was created. Another respect in which he stands apart from conventional aspects of coolness is his privileged background, as it was detailed by Fleming, who was an Old Etonian.

One of cool's innovations was to favour working-class integrity over aristocratic superiority. So it's notable that the actors who have played Bond most successfully are those with the least elitist demeanours. Fleming described Sean Connery as resembling an 'overdeveloped stuntman', while the appearance of Daniel Craig, who has recently saved the franchise from extinction, has been entertainingly compared to that of an 'angry waiter'. The suave Roger Moore also enjoyed success in the role, but it's Connery and Craig, the sons of a lorry driver and publican respectively, who have done most to make the Bond films one of the biggest properties in Hollywood history.

Nomads

Troubadours

When I told my brother I was writing this book, he mockingly observed that he imagined it would largely be devoted to singer-songwriters such as Bob Dylan*. And while that's not entirely true, you could make the case that being a singer-songwriter is the coolest occupation. You're not, like an actor, performing other people's material. You're not, like a novelist, hunched over a laptop for months on end, with little recompense to look forward to except the occasional enthusiastic Amazon review. The singer-songwriter produces and performs their own material, and, by and large, decides how it should be performed. In other words, they have more control over their work than any other creative artist. And they tour.

The rise of internet piracy has decimated the money made from music sales, leaving only live performance immune. The result is that musicians now tour more than ever, taking their place in a tradition that goes back to Ancient Greece. It was thanks to travelling *rhapsodes* that the stories of *The Iliad* and *The Odyssey* were preserved during a 300-year period when literacy had been lost. Bards in medieval Ireland were valued for their praise and feared for the toxicity of their satires, which were said to have the power, if the bard had been particularly riled, to raise boils on the faces of their victims. There is even an argument that itinerant musicians in the Provence region of France in the early Middle Ages, who were known as troubadours, somehow invented love. The theory goes that our modern idea of love with a capital L – the obsessive but ennobling passion, which entails sacrifice and pain, the fever that can strike at a glance, the transformation – was essentially a conceit dreamed up and developed by a bunch of Gallic singer-songwriters a thousand years ago.

The medieval troubadours travelled when they had to. Our modern-day equivalents do so because they can. It's part of the attraction, a double-edged ideal, solitary and romantic, but more celebrated than lamented. J.J. Cale's 1976 album *Troubadour* is a direct example; or one might think of London's Troubadour café, which has hosted performances by the likes of Bob Dylan, Jimi Hendrix* and Robert Plant. Or think, for other examples, of the Muddy Waters song 'Rollin' Stone'; the music magazine *Rolling Stone*; and the band the Rolling Stones.

Beatniks

In the 1920s, the novelist Gertrude Stein coined the phrase the 'Lost Generation' to describe men who were emotionally scarred by their experiences in the First World War. The 'Beat Generation' was the post-Second World War equivalent. In an early instance of a trend in cool slang, the natural meaning of the word 'beat' was reversed. True, it meant that the new generation was 'beat' as in bruised. But as adapted by Jack Kerouac* and others, who applied it to themselves, it also implied that they were *not* defeated. They were beaten-up, but not beaten. 'To be beat is to be at the bottom of your personality, looking up,' said the journalist John Clellon Holmes, who helped popularise the term. The Catholic Kerouac also associated it with the word 'beatific'. The Beats – or the Beatniks, as they came to be called – were on a quest for nothing less than heaven on earth.

They searched for it in artistic inspiration, drugs and spirituality, and in restless and relentless motion. The Beat movement was a movement about movement. The most obvious expression of the ideal was the first in what might be called the Synoptic Gospels of the Beatniks, Kerouac's autobiographical novel *On the Road* (1957), which sings the praises of the rootless existence. Apparently offended by the staid and sedentary nature of writing, the author even sought to make the act of literary creation kinetic by writing away like crazy in marathon stints, typing up his masterpiece (or so he claimed) onto a scroll of paper, which spooled across the floor of his room.

Allen Ginsberg's* long, ecstatic poem *Howl* – for all its profanity, a second sacred Beatnik text – became famous after being not published but physically performed one legendary night at the Six Gallery in San Francisco in 1955. As he declaimed it, the poet is said to have swayed rhythmically from side to side, while Kerouac in the audience banged his jug of cheap wine on the table, shouting 'Go!' at the turn of every line, as audience members did at jazz clubs. By the end, many of those present were in tears.

The third Beatnik gospel was William S. Burroughs'* *Naked Lunch* (1959), which he was able to write only after he had crossed the Atlantic ocean to Tangier* and Paris. It was Burroughs, too, who summed up the way the Beatnik ideal became commodified, sold and therefore cheapened, when he observed that *On the Road* had shifted 'a trillion pairs of Levis and a million espresso coffee machines'. In a small-scale version of a larger pattern, Beat-ism was trivialised by cash-ins such as *The Beat Generation Cookbook* as early as 1961. 'Eat Beat!' the book recommended, before detailing a catalogue of inexpensive recipes, affordable to anyone on their uppers. These included instructions for making 'Ginsbergers'.

Mobos

In the beginning, a rootless existence was the norm. The hunter-gatherer and herdsman moved from place to place. It was the practice of arable farming that ushered in the sedentary life. Yet the nomadic approach has survived to the present day in curious and distorted forms. Romany gypsies – descended, legend has it, from a cursed band of wandering lute-players – became known to some as Bohemians (owing to a mistaken belief that they had travelled to France via Bohemia in what is now the Czech Republic). The name 'bohemians' would later attach to arty types who lived and looked a bit like gypsies (favouring long hair and colourful clothes, for instance). In the 1990s, this was shortened to 'bohos', applied particularly to those from well-off backgrounds. This in turn has given rise to the term 'mobos', short for mobile bohemians, to describe bohos who roam the world, their laptops in their backpacks.

If this all seems a little confusing, that's because it is. Bohemians didn't necessarily stay on the move, like gypsies (although some did, such as the English painter Augustus John). Often bohos aren't especially creative. They just look as if they are. The same is true of mobos. The reason why artists embraced the gypsy lifestyle was because they could. An artist didn't have to dress smartly and could paint almost anywhere. What has changed is that, since the arrival of mobile phones and the internet, along with cheap travel and globalisation, that option is no longer open only to artists. Anyone whose work can be conducted entirely by email and phone call can live more or less wherever on the planet they choose.

This is not always all it's cracked up to be, as I can attest. During an experimental period after I moved to the Greek island of Corfu, I took my laptop down to the beach to write my weekly article, and tried to compose it while perched on a rock. It soon became clear this was completely impractical. So, much as mobos may tell themselves they're free spirits, they find themselves doing much of their work at a desk in a room, as they would in any city. The difference, perhaps, is the view. And what they can do in their downtime.

The truth

Method acting

One morning, during the filming of the 1975 Hollywood thriller *Marathon Man*, Dustin Hoffman staggered on set, his face haggard, his hair rearing up like a herd of wild horses. 'I've been awake all night preparing for this role,' he explained to his co-star, Laurence Olivier. 'My dear boy,' the great stage actor remonstrated, 'why don't you try *acting*?' This anecdote is often repeated, since people love the idea of the older man skewering the pretentiousness of the younger. For Hoffman's 'Method' approach to acting, going to huge lengths to invest his performance with an air of authenticity, is thought to be on the pretentious side. But if Olivier triumphed in that particular verbal skirmish, the war between old-fashioned 'surface' theatrical acting, and the movie depth and intensity associated with the more modern practice of the Method, has clearly been won by the likes of Hoffman.

The introduction of Method realism into acting in the 20th century had an electrifying effect. Pioneered by the Russian Constantin Stanislavski, and developed by Lee Strasberg and Stella Adler in New York, the new techniques – which placed the emphasis on intensive research and preparation before tackling a role, and a monomaniacal focus while playing it – produced an irresistible army of performers including Marlon Brando*, James Dean*, Robert De Niro* and Hoffman himself. What made it seem cool was that it not only constituted a rejection of tradition, but also gave actors greater kudos as artists than ever before, by virtue of the suffering they endured. Examples include the training De Niro underwent to play the boxer Jake LaMotta in *Raging Bull* (1980), to the point at which LaMotta himself declared that the actor could have turned pro. There are also competitive claims for the most weight lost or gained to play a part. De Niro put on 60lb for his later scenes in *Raging Bull*, but Christian Bale went two better, shedding 62lb for his role in 2004's *The Machinist*.

More recently, breakthroughs in the sophistication of CGI have had the effect, oddly enough, of making us less impressed by spectacle. Since anything can be faked, we hunger for some hint or glint of authenticity. It's provided by extreme instances of Method, with anecdotes leaked by publicists about the lengths actors have gone to for their performances. Think, for example, of the stories surrounding the making of *The Revenant*. Leonardo DiCaprio's performance must be good and truthful, we were encouraged to think, because he really ate that raw bison liver.

Given the close association claimed by Method practitioners with 'the truth', it's disconcerting to learn that the *Marathon Man* anecdote may not, after all, have been entirely true. Or rather, it has been misrepresented. The underlying truth, according to Hoffman, was that he was going through a painful marriage break-up at the time and had thrown himself into his work as a means of escape from the emotional pain. Olivier understood this and was worried about him. His suggestion that Hoffman should 'try acting', therefore, wasn't intended as a put-down. It was just a gentle suggestion that, on this occasion at least, perhaps he should take it easy.

Documentaries

Movies were born as documentaries. At first, they were called 'actuality films', an oft-cited early instance being the Lumière brothers' footage of a train arriving at a station, which when it was shown in 1898 is said to have sparked a panic among the audience, who feared they were about to be hit by the oncoming steam engine. Movie-makers have striven ever since to create equivalent sensations. Since the incredible advances in CGI and 3D effects of the 1990s, which make it possible to show whole cities being convincingly destroyed by natural or unnatural forces, Hollywood has been dominated by big-budget spectaculars, especially superhero operas such as the *Batman* and *Avengers* franchises.

Meanwhile, beneath the radar, documentaries have been making a quiet but confident comeback. The number of such films released in cinemas annually has increased exponentially over the past decade and a half. Four came out in the UK in 2001; 86 in 2012. This trend has been driven by a range of factors. Documentaries are the cheapest kind of film to make, and the new affordability of digital cameras has made that a viable option for more aspirant movie-makers than ever. Dwindling newspaper circulations, meanwhile, have greatly reduced the resources available to fund serious investigative journalism. Documentaries have picked up the slack. What we're driving at here is a renewed desire for something that might be termed 'the truth': an appetite that may presumably be increased by the tiresome barrage of big-budget nonsense to which Hollywood now devotes so much time and talent.

An aura of 'coolness' has attached to the form, being partly a lunar reflection of the light given off by the truth. Partly, too, it's the underdog vibe. The scruffy film-maker (Michael Moore, say) plays the role of a liberal left-wing David, slouching off on the trail of some sacred right-wing Goliath, whether it's big business or the gun lobby or whomever. It's striking that two of the films nominated for the Best Documentary Film Oscar in 2016 were studies of 'cool' singers (Amy Winehouse and Nina Simone*). The oeuvre of the iconoclastic documentary-maker Alex Gibney, as well as works devoted to Enron and Lance Armstrong, also includes films about Jimi Hendrix*, Hunter S. Thompson* and Wikileaks*.

Wikileaks

The internet is generally thought to be cool because, while it allows governments unprecedented access to the hopes and fears of their citizens, it also allows the reverse. The freedom of information has become so free, and perceived as such an inalienable right, that it has become harder than ever for the powers that be to keep the powerless in the dark. Wikipedia is an example: the free encyclopaedia, written and edited by the public, which offers anyone with internet access a breadth of information that once could only have been dreamed of. Another is the website Wikileaks. As the name suggests, it's a sort of Wikipedia, but one devoted to classified information, which has been leaked anonymously by whistle-blowers.

The website's Australian founder, the unusual-looking Julian Assange, with his pale skin and paler hair, has cast himself as a 21st-century Robin Hood, stealing information from the overlords and making it available to the underdogs (which is to say, us). Material published on the site includes documentation of toxic waste dumping on the Ivory Coast, manuals used by Scientologists, and most notoriously, classified military information, of a sometimes chilling nature, relating to the conduct of wars in Afghanistan and Iraq. As a man engaged in a moral crusade, Assange was always liable to be judged morally, and it has been here, on a personal and professional level, that he has got into trouble. Professionally, he has been willing to engage in techniques of secrecy similar to those against which he has campaigned. At one point, it's reported, he urged his employees to sign punitive non-disclosure forms.

In 2010, two women in Sweden accused Assange of sexual molestation. He has resisted extradition to stand trial in that country, instead embracing the immunity of residence in the Ecuadorian Embassy in London, where he remains at the time of writing. Some would say that the questions surrounding Assange's private life have no bearing on his achievements with Wikileaks. He himself has conflated the two, hinting that his accusers may have been bribed by his victims. Once, the welcome page of Wikileaks greeted visitors with a quote from the Buddha: 'Three things cannot hide for long: the Sun, the Moon and the truth.' If that's the case, then it won't be long before the truth about Julian Assange will come out.

Affectlessness

Irony

One of the ironic things about irony is that no one really knows what it is. Which is the aim of irony: to leave everyone in a state of paranoid confusion. Alanis Morissette clearly didn't know what it was when she penned her 1996 hit 'Ironic', since it was apparent she thought irony was when something annoying happens unexpectedly (rain on your wedding day, etc.). What confuses matters further is that the meaning of words isn't a constant. If enough people use a word in the 'wrong' way, it becomes right. And so many now use the word 'ironic' in the Morissette sense of 'unexpectedly annoying', it no longer seems as glaringly wrong as it did back in the 1990s. And isn't that, when you come to think of it, ironic?

Hell, who are we kidding? Morissette was just wrong. She'll always be wrong. Rain on your wedding day has nothing whatsoever to do with irony. No, irony is when someone announces (as in Sophocles' *Oedipus Tyrannus*) that they're going to track down a murderer, only to discover they unknowingly committed the crime themselves. That's what's known as dramatic irony. Even that, though, isn't what we're interested in here, which is tonal irony, a way of speaking or writing so it's hard to be sure whether or not you're being serious. The word 'irony' originally comes from *eiron*, used to describe a stock character in Ancient Greek comedies who would pretend to be more stupid or weaker than they were in reality. They knew the truth. We in the audience knew the truth. But the other characters, often, didn't. This is a key aspect of irony, as it is of cool: the idea that some get it and some don't.

The 'eiron' figure finds his cool descendants in the character of Hamlet*, who pretends to be mad but isn't, and that played by Humphrey Bogart* in *Casablanca*, who pretends to be amoral but is actually noble. More generally, the cool cat deals in humour, while preserving a deadpan mien, which makes it almost impossible to tell what he or she is really thinking or feeling. This is open to abuse. It can be used as an insurance policy, so you're covered if you ever accidentally say anything crass or stupid; you were merely being ironic. Worse, it can be used as a tool of power. If no one knows your meaning or intent, they feel insecure, while you keep the whip hand. And that's just not cool, is it. Is it, though.

Postmodernism

The postmodernist condition is to be unsure about everything, including the meaning of postmodernism (cf. the ironic thing about irony*). Clearly, this was something that happened *after* modernism. So far, so good. Modernism was the attempt to create a new art and literature that would make sense of the tectonic upheavals of modernity. Postmodernism questions the notion of making sense of anything. It was developed by left-wing academics such as Jean-François Lyotard, who were so disappointed by the failure of Marxism that they rejected all 'grand narratives'. A classic work of historical postmodernism was Francis Fukuyama's *The End of History* (1992), which argued that we had reached a point of completion: democracy had won, capitalism was the way forward, peace had conquered war. The book is now something of a historical curiosity, yet postmodernism's influence remains.

What's cool about it? In broad terms, it rejects the value pillars on which people have constructed their understanding of the world. Love? A social construct. Morality? Ditto. Truth? A lie, say the postmodernists. There is not space here, fortunately, to grapple with the epistemological complexities of these claims. But what we can both see and say is that philosophical postmodernism has given birth to an accompanying artistic style, which involves sudden tonal shifts (from horror to comedy, say), which favours the ludic over the lucid, and which finds ways to question the very meaning of love, morality and truth. The last of these may, for instance, be undermined by multiple-perspective narratives, in which the truth not only looks but is different depending on viewpoint. Akira Kurosawa's *Rashomon* is a classic example in cinema. In literature, Lawrence Durrell's *Alexandria Quartet* tried a similar trick.

As a rule of thumb, postmodernist architecture is architecture that doesn't look like architecture (such as the works of Frank Gehry) and postmodernist art is art that doesn't look like art (such as the works of Jeff Koons). There are some who say that postmodernism is dead and that we are now in an age of post-postmodernism, but it's not obvious what that could mean except that postmodernism isn't as trendy as it was. It's still quite trendy though, with acclaimed artists and film-makers continuing to work in a postmodernist style of coolness, especially in the emotional (or emotionless) sense of the word. If you really believe that love, morality and truth are social constructs, there's nothing much to get worked up about.

Poker

There are two reasons why poker has acquired its cool reputation. The first is that it requires players to maintain a 'poker face', controlling their emotions to the extent that no one else around the table can tell if they are holding a good hand. But that could be said, to some degree, of other card games too. The second reason, then, is the clincher: that in poker it's possible to win by bluffing, by increasing your stake as if you had a good hand, and convincing your opponents to back down. Pull off this trick and you confirm the truth of Paul Newman's* remark in the film *Cool Hand Luke* (1967) when he observes, after bluffing his way to victory in a poker game, that sometimes 'nothing' can be a 'real cool hand'.

It isn't easy to make a game of cards cinematically exciting. Part of the problem is that you can't rely on the audience knowing the rules, so there usually has to be an awkward exchange on the periphery of the game, in which one spectator (usually a man) explains to another (usually a woman) what's going on. Nevertheless, such is poker's allure that many have tried to produce a great poker movie, with honourable attempts including *The Cincinnati Kid* (1965) and *The Sting* (1973), and more recently *Rounders* (1998).

The fact that a game will often reduce to two men facing off across the baize has encouraged a thickly macho air to proceedings. The jargon of play is staccato with monosyllables. 'Stud', 'check', 'burn', 'call', 'fold', 'flop', and so on. It's the kind of game where you don't say, 'He's slow but steady.' You say, 'He's a grinder.' Money is thrown around, but it's not about the money. Or at least it's important to act as if it's not. After triumphing in the world championship in 1981, the legendary Stu Ungar was asked what he planned to do with his considerable prize. 'Lose it,' the legend replied. He could say that, because he had won, and what poker is really about is sorting the winners from the losers. Among the myths that players like to tout is that there is 'a sucker' at every table. And as it's often observed, if you haven't worked out after half an hour who the sucker is, then the sucker is you.

Parodies

The Fonz

There's a scene in Quentin Tarantino's* 1994 movie *Pulp Fiction** in which the gangster* played by Samuel L. Jackson has a stand-off with two robbers in a restaurant. He points his gun at one of them. The other one points her gun at him. Jackson insists they're all going to be like 'three little Fonzies'. To clarify his meaning, he asks her what 'Fonzie' is like. Anyone who had ever watched the nostalgic American sitcom *Happy Days* during its TV run from 1974 to 1984 knew the answer to that one. Arthur Herbert Fonzarelli, better known as 'Fonzie' or 'The Fonz', was proverbially cool.

Sporting a black leather jacket, with an impeccable quiff of dark hair, The Fonz rarely betrayed an emotion beyond mild amusement or mild annoyance. If he wanted a girl, he had merely to click his fingers and one would appear on his arm as if by magic. A high-school drop-out who worked as a mechanic, he wielded an uncanny power over machinery. A broken-down car would miraculously start to purr if he gave it a smack (this knack became known as the 'Fonzie touch'). His party trick was to hit the juke box at the local drive-in, with the result that it would instantly launch into Elvis Presley's* *Hound Dog*. In response to which, The Fonz might give a double thumbs-up, accompanied by his trade-mark exclamation of 'Heeeey!'

The Fonz was an affectionate middle-brow parody of the edgy-but-relaxed style that had been defined as the meaning of cool in the 1950s by actors such as Marlon Brando*. Intended as a secondary character by the creators of *Happy Days*, he soon emerged as the star of the show, and the actor who played him, Henry Winkler, found himself globally famous. Bette Davis invited him for dinner. Orson Welles greeted him with the words, 'We finally meet.' He was even once contacted by police in Indiana and told there was a teenager intent on throwing himself off a building, who had said he would be willing to 'talk to Fonzie'. Winkler took the call. He played it cool, giving the boy a pep talk about the gift of life, and ultimately persuading him to step away from the edge.

The Dude

The 1998 Coen brothers movie *The Big Lebowski* is a parable about the power of coolness. It sets up its argument by having two characters called Jeffrey Lebowski, with contrasting personalities. The 'big' Lebowski (in the sense of being older and richer) is a wheelchair-bound plutocrat, a 'square' achiever, with a trophy wife who doesn't respect him. He plans a scam that involves screwing over the 'small' Lebowski, better known as 'The Dude', a 'cool' drop-out who doesn't mean anyone any harm. The film doesn't give The Dude an easy ride. He is regularly beaten up, for example, suggesting that his brand of countercultural 1970s pacifism isn't particularly practical for dealing with some of the problems that life throws at him.

On the other hand, The Dude, who is the film's hero, ultimately receives its endorsement. The narrator of the story, a Texan with a stetson and a huge drooping moustache, tells him he likes his style. It's a classic moment in cinema: the cowboy*, who lit the torch of coolness in early westerns, giving the nod to the hippy who took it up and carried it on. It's funny, too, that he likes his style, since the style of The Dude, as played by the majestic Jeff Bridges, is pretty sloppy. He slouches around in whatever clothes come to hand, sporting long hair, which he occasionally ties up with a hair clip when he wants to concentrate on what appears to be his only passion in life (apart from drinking White Russians and smoking spliffs), which is ten-pin bowling.

As a caricature of 1950s cool, The Fonz* achieved huge cultural currency. Ali G*, parodying 1990s street cool, also secured iconic status. The Dude, a relic of the 1970s, doesn't have such instant recognition value. The film wasn't even a critical or commercial hit when it came out. Yet over the years, it has achieved cult status. Literally. There is a tongue-in-cheek spiritual movement called Dudeism that is devoted to pursuing the hero's slacker life philosophy. For instance, it proudly declares itself 'the world's slowest-growing religion'. There's also a Lebowski Fest in LA, where the film is set. One of its main attractions, in addition to the chance to dress up like The Dude in a shabby cardigan and classic sunglasses, is a night of unlimited bowling. The London version of the festival is called The Dude Abides, quoting a famous line of dialogue. It is a sentence that sums up the movie's message. The 1960s dream may be over, but dudeness – also known as coolness – decidedly abides.

Ali G

Booyakasha! Sorry. If there's one thing we've learnt from Ali G's success it's that there's nothing more excruciating than a bad Ali G impersonation. Which is partly because he was so good, and so funny, in his first appearances at the end of the 1990s. As played by well-heeled Jewish comedian Sasha Baron Cohen, the character was an ignorant mixed-race English TV interviewer who was in love with black culture, and whose muddled identity flushed out our contemporary confusions. One of these was that because Ali G appeared to be 'cool', albeit in an absurdly parodic way, his interviewees were reluctant to call his bluff, and so risk seeming 'uncool'. His black or Asian pretensions also seemed to give him near-immunity from being challenged.

The best interviews were the earliest, when the interviewees had less chance of realising that they were being taken for a ride. Highlights included Ali G asking the left-wing politician Tony Benn if the reason the welfare state was so called was because it was 'well fair', and addressing Boutros Boutros Ghali, the former UN secretary-general, as 'Boutros

Boutros Boutros Ghali'. In many of these encounters, part of the joke was to see public figures so out of touch with youth culture they couldn't even tell when it was being sent up. The funnier Ali G became, though, the harder it got for him to be funny. In a classic instance of success eating itself, as soon as everyone knew who he was, he couldn't pull off undercover interviews any more. So he launched his own show, on which all the guests, inevitably, knew exactly what was going on. And that just wasn't as funny.

But think back to those early interviews: the time he mentioned to a bemused Buzz Aldrin that many conspiracy theorists* have suggested the Moon doesn't actually exist; or when he asked linguistics professor Noam Chomsky, 'How many words does you know? And what is some of dem?' The real miracle of these encounters, apart from Baron Cohen's nerve at forcing often quite serious people to have ridiculous conversations, was his ability to keep a straight face. That took some kind of incredible chutzpah. Respek! And indeed Booyakasha!

Places

Tangier

Tangier has a claim to being the most foreign city on the planet. Even in ancient times, its location at the north-west corner of Africa was regarded as being literally teetering on the world's brink. It was situated by the site of the fabled pillars of Hercules, which were said not only to support the sky, but also to be engraved with the words 'Nec plus ultra', meaning 'beyond this, nothing'. In the first half of the 20th century, the city's atmosphere was conditioned by the 'international zone' years, when it was controlled by a conglomerate of countries. By the time of Moroccan independence in 1956, the population was divided equally between Moroccans and non-Moroccans. In other words, it had become as foreign to locals as to foreigners.

Over the decades, the city where everyone feels out of place has had an irresistible allure for writers and other disenchanted types looking to escape from or find themselves. Often, it seems, you need to do the former before you can do the latter. Once in a bar in Tangier, a drunk woman who had been insulting Noël Coward explained that she was merely being herself. 'That's a thing you should never be,' he observed swiftly. The Beatnik author William S. Burroughs* had to move to Tangier before he was able to write his masterpiece,

Naked Lunch (1959), of which it could fairly be said, 'Nec plus ultra'. A sprawling, disturbing trip of drug-taking, gay sex and paranoid visions, it is arguably the most self-consciously 'cool' book that has ever been written.

The title was suggested to Burroughs by Jack Kerouac*, who visited him in Tangier. As did Allen Ginsberg*, who name-dropped the place in his cool checklist, the ecstatic poem *Howl*, praising those who went there for 'the boys'. For the Beatniks*, Tangier's attraction owed a lot to its promise of illicit drugs and sex with rent boys or prostitutes. That same glow drew Tennessee Williams*, Joe Orton and Truman Capote, among others. Anita Pallenberg* fled to Tangier with Keith Richards* in 1967, abandoning her drug-addled ex, Brian Jones, in Marrakech. It's a city for lovers running away, experimental authors, and anyone looking for a new (but not necessarily fresh) start. The novelist Paul Bowles said the difference between a tourist and a traveller is that the former doesn't expect to change. Some, such as Bowles himself and Christopher Gibbs*, embraced permanent change, settling for good or ill in the transit lounge of the world.

London

Interviewed for a self-consciously cool 1967 documentary*, David Hockney, wearing a pair of comedy thick-rimmed spectacles, declared in his flat, matter-of-fact northern accent that there was nothing remotely cool about London. The artist complained that everything closed early – unlike in LA, where he preferred to spend his time. He also slagged off Annabel's, the then-trendy Mayfair nightclub, complaining that the chairs were so small you felt you were at a children's tea party; and the drinks were absurdly overpriced, costing as much as £1 each. In the same documentary, the actress Julie Christie, by contrast, conceded that England's capital had probably become the coolest city in the world, suggesting that this was the result of the phenomenal success of The Beatles, which had drawn creative heat across the Atlantic from the US.

New York is the only serious rival to London's claim to have made the single greatest contribution of any city to the history of cool. Yet America's superpower status is something of a sticking point. Can you be cool, in the end, if you're in charge? The historian Dominic Sandbrook has recently argued (and he isn't the first) that Britain's cool status was precisely enabled by its slow then sudden loss of political power. Out of the debris of empire, the country reassembled itself as a 'dream factory', which is to say a world leader in the entertainment industries, with so-called 'Swinging London' as the hub. Displaced colonialist vocabulary was co-opted to describe it. The British influence became known as 'the British Invasion', and as well as pop groups, its ground troops included not only actors and artists such as Hockney and Christie, but also gallerists and hairdressers, fashion designers and interior decorators.

At intervals, some professional controversialist will write an article declaring that London is dead. Creative types have been priced out of the property market, the argument runs, leaving their former haunts occupied by bohos and bankers. In truth, these dyspeptic middle-aged writers usually have in mind a couple of areas in particular – wherever it was they happened to spend their knockabout twenties. It's all non-sense, of course. The city's sprawling size, which means that whenever one postcode gets gentrified there's always another ready to assume the 'edgy' label, combined with the underdog irony and ceaseless tolerance of its inhabitants, makes its pos-ition seem pretty secure.

The Chelsea Hotel

Some hotels are faded. Some are positively disgusting. And then there's New York's Chelsea Hotel, which is inextric-ably associated with dankly peeling wallpaper and clanking, recalcitrant pipes. It was to here that the bloated poet Dylan Thomas slouched in the dead of night, mumbled to his mistress that he had just drunk eighteen straight whiskies, and promptly expired. On another occasion, during a fund-raising lunch, Jackson Pollock* drunkenly vomited on the Chelsea's carpet. On yet another, hammered, the novelists Jack Kerouac* and Gore Vidal decided they 'owed it to lit-erary history' (the phrase was Vidal's) to spend the night together, and checked into the Chelsea – where else? – to perform the laborious deed.

When it was designed in 1883 by the architect Philip Hubert, the place was intended to be a haven for artists, inspired by the utopian theories of Charles Fourier. And so it became, its high studios attracting painters with their promise of unencumbered light, the low rents appealing to authors and bohemians of every stripe. Arthur C. Clarke wrote *2001: A Space Odyssey* while staying at the Chelsea. Arthur Miller moved into room 614 after his divorce from Marilyn Monroe; Janis Joplin* slept with Leonard Cohen in 424; Sid Vicious stabbed his girlfriend Nancy Spungen to death in 100. William S. Burroughs*, Bob Dylan*, Jimi Hendrix* and Patti Smith* all hung out at the Chelsea at one time or another.

As a hotel, it attracted transients, and as an establishment run eccentrically for decades by manager Stanley Bard, it allowed them to do pretty much as they liked. The first floor was famously frequented by prostitutes. But because of its astonishing roll call of decadent and distinguished habitués, it continued to lure the pilgrims of cool long after its heyday. Madonna* posed there for some of the pictures for her book *Sex*. Luc Besson used it for interior locations when shooting his 1994 action thriller *Léon*. In more recent years, it has hosted such notable cool-chasers as the actor Ethan Hawke and the British post-punk rock group The Libertines. In 2007, Bard was finally ousted as manager, and four years later the hotel was closed for refurbishment. It is scheduled to reopen in 2017, although whether its anarchic spirit will survive the removal of the mould and the mice remains to be seen.

Heroes

Cowboys

Once upon a time in Hollywood, westerns were the most popular movie genre, accounting for a quarter of all films made. For they chimed with a founding myth of America: the narrative of white European pioneers carving a civilisation out of the wilderness. At first, too, it was the fact that, in the silent-movie era, they gave scope for action with an immediately recognisable visual language: the majestic scenery, the circle of wagons attacked by whooping savages, the skilled gunman who leads a heroic resistance. This dazzling figure – also known as a cowboy since he was basically a pistol-packing herdsman – provided a template for the cool hero at the movies until the 1960s.

It was itself inspired by the knight errant of medieval literature, who had wandered a desolate landscape (on horseback, as the cowboy would be), righting wrongs and rescuing damsels in distress. America's early self-image was as the underdog who had defeated its overlord in the form of imperialist Britain: an idea that also found resonance in the person of the downbeat but undefeated cowboy. Yet with the country's rise to superpower status by the mid-20th century, it was a note that ceased to ring so pure and true. The coolness that the movie cowboy had helped to create now began to turn on him. Viewed through the countercultural prism, the cowboy seemed merely the hired thug of a disguised imperialist: the European invader stealing land from the Native American. The popularity of the western went into decline, entering a silver age of lurid sub-genres such as ultra-violent spaghetti westerns (*A Fistful of Dollars*), spoofs (*Blazing Saddles*), and revisionist apologies (*Dances With Wolves*).

A couple of recent examples illustrate the change. In the original film of *The Magnificent Seven** (1960), the heroes were predominantly white, whereas in the 2016 remake, they include a Korean, a Mexican, a black American and a Native American. Or consider 2013's *The Lone Ranger*, in which the biggest-name star, Johnny Depp, played not the fearless lawman, but his Native American sidekick, Tonto (the film itself seeking to redress a cultural wrong by giving the Native American a more prominent role than the white man). But that film appears to have missed at least one historical trick. The eponymous ranger, who has always been portrayed onscreen by a white actor, seems originally to have been based on a historical figure who was black – an Arkansas-born lawman named Bass Reeves, reported to have captured or killed 3,000 felons without ever getting shot.

Private eyes

When the Pinkerton National Detective Agency was founded in 1850, its motto – 'We never sleep' – was displayed beneath the emblem of an unblinking eye. Hence the origin of the phrase 'private eye' to describe a private detective. From the earliest days, it was not an entirely respectable profession. The first known example of the type, the Frenchman Eugène François Vidocq, was arrested in 1842 for taking money on false pretences. Yet thanks to the alchemy of Hollywood, the private eye acquired an edgy glamour, as personified by the fictitious detectives Sam Spade and Philip Marlowe, who appeared in the films *The Maltese Falcon* (1941) and *The Big Sleep* (1946), in both cases played by Humphrey Bogart*.

The first movie was an adaptation of the novel by Dashiell Hammett, an author who once described the figure of the private eye as 'a dream man', not in the Sherlock Holmes* sense of possessing supernaturally perceptive faculties, but as 'a hard and shifty fellow, able to take care of himself in any situation'. *Pace* Hammett, the Holmes factor may presumably be a part of the profession's appeal. But about the tough-guy image he's persuasive. The private eye of film noir is usually, if not a psychopath, at least a hard-nut. He also has a quip ready for all occasions, especially in the case of Philip Marlowe, thanks to the flamboyant wit of the author Raymond Chandler, who created him in a series of novels.

The private eye operates outside the law, beholden to none. He's keen on his pay cheque and has a weakness for dames, especially blondes. This penchant is well expressed by Marlowe in *Farewell, My Lovely*, who on first sighting a female client notes appreciatively, 'She was a blonde to make a bishop kick a hole in a stained-glass window.' If this all sounds a little too good to be true, that's because it is. In reality, the profession remains as tawdry as ever. Today's private eye spends most of his or her time trying to dig up dirt on one rampant capitalist to benefit another, or attempting to undermine 'Workers' Comp' cases (when someone claims to have been injured at work), or investigating possible marital infidelity. When I spoke to one London-based private eye, he told me that if someone suspects their spouse of cheating on them, they are nearly always right. Which is depressing, if true. But of course, it would be in the interests of the private eye to claim it was true, even if it wasn't.

Geeks

When I was at school with Benedict Cumberbatch in the early 1990s, there was a widespread feeling that, although very talented, he was unlikely to make it as a professional actor in the long run. For one thing, he didn't have conventional leading-man looks. And he was too much of a geek. Of course, we were a bunch of teenagers, so what did we know? Not much, clearly. One thing we failed to predict was the communications revolution, one of the consequences of which has been that to seem tech-savvy, and more generally science-minded – in other words, to be a geek – has become a social advantage. Geekdom is now the new cool and Benedict Cumberbatch is its geeky-suave poster child.

The word 'geek' was originally used to describe circus performers, oddball simpletons whose speciality was to bite the heads off chickens. By the 1980s, the word's sense had shifted to mean someone nerdishly obsessed with computers. It's only in the last decade or so that it has been elevated to a label to be brandished with pride, a transition that has been marked out by the trajectory of Cumberbatch's career: his tousle-haired Sherlock Holmes* in the TV show *Sherlock* (launched 2010); his oddly accented Wikileaks* founder Julian Assange in *The Fifth Estate* (2013); the ascetic scientist Alan Turing in *The Imitation Game* (2014). What those characters have in common, at least in his portrayals, is they all apparently suffer from a mild form of Asperger syndrome. They find social interaction hard. They interpret language literally. They fail to demonstrate what are regarded as the normal emotional responses. This extreme form of the geek hero – what you might call the 'Asperger hero' – is cropping up all over the place now in TV and cinema. Other examples include the robustly strange heroine of the TV drama *The Bridge* (launched 2011) and the intense, twitchy hedge fund manager Michael Burry in *The Big Short* (2015).

The argument, then, is that left-wing cool was neutralised in the capitalist 1980s, mugged and left for dead. It groggily came round in the 1990s, in rave culture, grunge and Britpop, but it proved a temporary nostalgia. The revival guttered, leading us to a tentative conclusion. If there is hope, it lies in the geeks. These are the disciples and descendants of the triumvirate of the communication age, Bill Gates, Steve Jobs* and Mark Zuckerberg, the men who founded Microsoft, Apple and Facebook respectively, and in the process reshaped our world.

Villains

Pirates

When the suits at Disney cast Johnny Depp as Captain Jack Sparrow in their film *Pirates of the Caribbean*, they were hoping he'd deliver a traditional swashbuckler in the Burt Lancaster mode. But Depp was having none of it. After pondering the matter, he latched onto the idea that pirates had been the rock stars of their day. Accordingly he decided that in the movie he would channel the spirit and mannerisms of his friend, the Rolling Stones guitarist Keith Richards*. Watching early rushes of the film, the execs were appalled. As Depp, covered in jewellery and heavy goth make-up, teetered and mugged, they asked one another: is he drunk? Or, worse, is he pretending to be gay? When this was put to him, the actor had a nice riposte. 'Didn't you know?' he replied innocently. '*All* my characters are gay.' As it turned out, he was on the money. An endearing blend of courage and cowardice, apparent amorality and wry romanticism, his rock 'n' roll pirate has become one of the iconic modern movie characters.

Booty, wenches, rum. The appeal of the piratical life isn't hard to see. In reality, of course, life on the seven seas was most likely a living hell, and most pirates, unlike Captain Jack Sparrow, must have been utter bastards. One possible exception, oddly enough, is the privateer known as Blackbeard (real name: Edward Teach). This is despite the fact that his image couldn't have been more terrifying. According to an exuberant 18th-century account, his beard, which 'came up to his eyes', resembled 'a frightful meteor'. When boarding another ship, he used to strap six pistols to his chest, grip a cutlass in either hand, and trail lit fuses from beneath his hat, so that fumes wreathed his head like smoke from the depths of hell. Once, it's reported, he tried to shoot one of his shipmates for insubordination. He missed and struck his second-in-command, Israel Hands, in the knee. The apologetic buccaneer explained that if he didn't execute one of his crew every now and then, they would forget who he was. Yet historians have argued that Blackbeard may actually have been a relatively decent cove, who cultivated his fearsome reputation precisely in order that he wouldn't have to kill anyone. Ships simply surrendered at his approach.

If you're still unconvinced about the importance of pirates to our theme, bear in mind the swashbuckling heroes the poet Lord Byron* created to develop his pre-cool persona in his bestselling poems (back in the days when the latter phrase wasn't a contradiction in terms). And consider, then, the three major movies that have been made about the mutiny on HMS *Bounty*. The historical facts are that during a trip to Tahiti for breadfruit in 1789, the master's mate, Fletcher Christian, turned pirate when he seized control of that ship from its captain, William Bligh. In each of the films, the rebellious Christian was played by an actor who was then considered possibly the coolest man on the planet: Clark Gable in 1935, Marlon Brando* in 1962, and Mel Gibson in 1984. The first two films emphasised the tyrannical cruelty of Captain Bligh, justifying the actions of a coolly subversive Christian. The third offers a more ambiguous view. Yet all three present a pretty dashing vision of the master's mate. It should be noted, however, that the real-life Bligh described the real-life Christian as 'bow-legged' and prone to 'violent perspiration, particularly in his hands, so that he soils anything he handles'.

Gangsters

The supposed coolness of gangsters is so ingrained in our consciousness, it seems sacrilegious to question it. As with the cinematic presentation of pirates*, anyone seeking confirmation that it's a cool role needs only to read the roll call. The 'godfather' of the gang, fittingly enough, is the Godfather himself, the titular don of Mario Puzo's novel, who in his screen incarnation took the thick-set form of Marlon Brando*, exaggerating the cloudiness of his already muffled diction by tucking pieces of cotton wool inside his cheeks. There's a great moment in that movie when the pop star and movie heart-throb Johnny Fontaine comes to the don moaning about how he needs a certain film role or he's finished. Brando grabs him and shakes him, telling him to 'act like a man'. Forget the posturing of singers and actors, the scene seems to say. When it comes to cool, gangsters are the real deal.

By 'gangsters', in this context, we mainly mean Italian American mafiosi. The rise of this strain of thuggery came about in the US after Italy's new leader Benito Mussolini enforced a crackdown on crime. A wave of Italian migrants crossed the Atlantic to evade the police back home. Around the same time, the prohibition of alcohol set up the conditions for bootlegging and protection rackets. Power and wealth accrued to criminal kingpins such as Al Capone in Chicago. In person, the latter was a show-off, encrusting his corpulent form with jewellery. He always turned to one side when photographed, to conceal a scar he'd received from a man whose sister he had inadvertently insulted. There was nothing cool about that. In the end, Capone was put away for tax evasion. He deserved worse, but at the same time there seems something pleasingly uncool about the prosaic charge he went down for.

The inherent *uncoolness* of gangsters is arguably contained within the word itself. By definition, a gangster belongs to a gang. A solitary gangster is a contradiction in terms. So after rejecting one set of rules, those of conventional society, the gangster slavishly conforms to those of his gang. In the case of mafiosi, these famously include the principle of *omertà*: you don't rat on another member of your 'family'. Which is all very well, but it has so often been broken in practice as to have rather lost its mystique.

Vampires

'Sleep all day. Party all night. Never grow old. Never die. It's fun to be a vampire.' So ran the promotional tagline for the 1987 teen movie *The Lost Boys*, in which Kiefer Sutherland played the charismatic leader of a leather-clad gang of California bikers whose dark secret was that they were also bloodsucking vampires. It was, in other words, a juvenile delinquency film (cf. Marlon Brando* in *The Wild One*), but with fangs. Perhaps it helps to have grown up in the 1980s if you really want to regard the film as a classic, but to the extent that the idea succeeds, it's thanks to the obvious coolness of vampires, who not only never grow old but also never grow up. Hence the film's title.

Before the invention of cool in the mid-20th century, vampires weren't generally regarded as sexy rebels. Quite the contrary. They were gloomy or ghoulish creatures, walking cadavers, with about as much sex appeal as that implies. The bloodsucker myth originated in the Middle Ages out of ignorance about the natural processes of posthumous decomposition: the fact that nails and hair continue to grow, and blood and other fluids may ooze from orifices, including the mouth. In other words, sometimes a corpse would have blood around its lips. Imagination did the rest.

Creeping, drooling, generally disgusting monsters at first, vampires were later reinvented as urbane middle-European aristocrats by Bram Stoker in his sensational, sensationalist 1897 novel *Dracula*. More recent decades have seen various new spins on the vampire story. Among the most recent is the doomed romantic bloodsucker played by Robert Pattinson in the *Twilight* franchise (which, like *The Lost Boys*, exploits the similarities between moody teenagers and supernatural demons with overgrown canines). The distinguishing feature here is that Pattinson doesn't want to be a vampire. His condition is a contagious curse, like a diabolical form of STD, from which he nobly wishes to protect his girlfriend (Kristen Stewart). From being emblematic of depraved clergy or corrupt aristocracy, or embodying fears of the effects of Eastern European immigration, the vampire myth became a parable about the importance of practising safe sex.

Counter-examples

To my teenage self, the shouty lead singer of the Irish stadium rock band U2, his hooded eyes forever swathed in wrap-around shades, seemed seriously cool. *Achtung Baby* had just come out: an agile, industrial-sounding album with some apparently edgy, Berlin-set sleeve artwork. What wasn't to like? Which is why it has grieved me so much over the years, my gradual realisation that Bono is generally regarded as an 'eejit' (to use the Irish term). In the year of *Achtung Baby*'s release, the disrespectful pop stars The Pet Shop Boys took the piss with a disco cover version of the U2 anthem 'Where the Streets Have No Name'. Getting rid of the guitar bombast left the grandiose lyrics embarrassingly exposed: vague stuff about oppressive walls and wanting to reach out and 'touch the flame'. After Bono heard the travesty, he responded with a reference to a well-known Pet Shop Boys hit, asking, 'What have I, what have I, what have I done to deserve this?' (You see? *He* can be funny too.) But that's the question. What had he done?

The answer seems to run as follows. In our permissive society, in which almost anything is allowed, nothing annoys people more than being told how to behave. In other words, whatever you do, don't preach. Bono is a preacher. He's drawn

161

to a pulpit with an irresistible compulsion, taking time out from touring to tell us why he thinks we should cancel Third World debt, for instance, or all join forces to tackle the AIDS epidemic in Africa. Another key point is that a lot of people think U2's music is crap. The only thing worse than being told how to behave by a rock star is being told how to behave by a crap rock star. And as everyone knows, you can't argue about taste.

There's something a little queasy, for sure, about mixing pop music with politics. When Bono referred to Tony Blair* and Gordon Brown as 'the John and Paul of the global-development stage', it was a low moment. As was his sunglasses-swapping with the Pope. (Maybe you *can* argue about taste, after all.) More seriously, he stands accused of hypocrisy because he tells rich nations to forget their debts, while going out of his way to avoid paying tax in his native Ireland. The gravest indictment, though, is that he pushes the wrong solutions to the problems he preaches about. This blend of perceived qualities – preachiness, musical pomposity, vulgarity, hypocrisy and wrong-headedness when intervening in matters of life and death – adds up to a heavy charge sheet. I could try to defend him, but it would be about as advisable as trying to touch a flame.

Tom Cruise

In the 1986 action movie *Top Gun*, the fighter pilots all have nicknames that tell you exactly what they're like. Maverick, played by Tom Cruise, is (cough) a maverick. Goose is a bit silly. Iceman is as cool as ice. (It was never entirely clear what we were meant to make of Slider.) But we could see that in the coolness stakes, the prize was taken by Maverick, the rebellious outsider. Although on the short side, he was dashing, with a nose just large enough to make his face interesting. When he wasn't wrestling with internal demons, his dazzling grin suggested that he was having fun, and would be fun to hang out with.

As an actor, Cruise embodied the cocky charisma of shiny 1980s capitalism. Yet it was in the 1990s that he played his most interesting roles, among them a stressed-out sports agent in *Jerry Maguire* (1996) and a misogynistic motivational speaker in *Magnolia* (1999). Yet behind the scenes, his private life was complicated, to say the least. Poor Tom. Having been an actor since his teens, he longed for answers to life's deeper questions. He just picked really badly. Scientology is founded on a bizarre mythology involving aliens being blown up inside volcanoes, who later … But there's no point trying to make sense of it. And it was tough for Cruise, because the gulf between his charismatic image and his controversial, Scientology-inspired views (for instance, dismissing all psychiatry as pseudoscience) was widening. His megawatt smile started to look strained in interviews. He began to laugh too loud and long.

In his book *Going Clear*, the Pulitzer-winning author Lawrence Wright asserts that the actor's fellow Scientologists made use of information gleaned from supposedly private therapy sessions to pick him a suitable girlfriend from among their ranks. That relationship didn't last. With two marriages behind him – to actress Mimi Rogers, who introduced him to Scientology, and actress Nicole Kidman – Cruise boldly got engaged to another actress, Katie Holmes. His sang-froid cracked during a 2005 interview with Oprah Winfrey when he bounced up and down on her sofa, declaring, 'I'm in love and it's one of those things where you want to be cool, like, "Yeah, I like her." That's not how I feel.' A talented movie star whose career remains surprisingly buoyant in spite of everything, Cruise seemed to reveal himself on that sofa. He was not only a maverick, we saw, but also a bit of a goose.

Tony Blair

In 1997, an issue of *Vanity Fair* proclaimed on its cover that 'London Swings Again!' The article within sang the praises of Britpop bands such as Blur and Oasis, Young British Artists such as Damien Hirst, and the 'shirt-sleeved, smiling' leader of the Labour party, Tony Blair. Coolness isn't really – it can't be – the business of politicians. If you're in charge, what can you conceivably be rebelling against? Yourself? But Labour had been out of power for so long, by 1997 the prospect of a change seemed pretty rock 'n' roll. This was an impression that Blair – who while at Oxford had fronted a rock band named Ugly Rumours, basing his style on that of Mick Jagger – expertly encouraged, with his compulsive ability to intuit whatever it was that people wished to hear.

By the 1990s scepticism about the trustworthiness of British politicians was endemic. As Britain's PM from 1997 to 2007, Blair presented himself as a man you could rely on. 'I think most people who have dealt with me,' he declared chummily in an early interview, 'think I'm a pretty straight sort of guy.' In his autobiography, he uses the phrase 'the truth is' 44 times. He was going to call the book *The Journey* but was persuaded that this sounded a little self-important, so changed it to *A Journey*. And there you have his personality-split between what the journalist Allison Pearson has called 'Messiah Tony' and 'bloke Tony'. It was similarly embodied in the moment when, shortly before announcing the Good Friday Agreement he had helped to broker in Ireland, he announced 'this is not a day for sound bites', before adding that he felt 'the hand of history' on his shoulder.

As a speaker he can be extraordinarily persuasive, but he's better in person than in print. There's nothing cool about the prose style of *A Journey*. The book includes unintended rhymes: the 'Iraqi hierarchy'. Portentous clichés: having committed to the invasion of Iraq, he declares, 'the die was cast'. Even odd imprecisions of language. 'We were at war,' he declares. 'How long, bloody and difficult was soon to become apparent.' But presumably none of those things was 'soon' apparent. Blair's chameleonic complaisance worked best when addressing a party conference. In his memoir, he doesn't know who might be reading it. In his desire to be all things to all readers, he dematerialises and disappears entirely.

Eastern spirituality

Hinduism

Sometimes described as the world's oldest religion, Hinduism isn't actually a religion in the same way as Christianity or Islam, but rather a collection of spiritual beliefs that arose in India over the centuries, out of which more exclusive 'founded' belief systems have emerged (Sikhism and Buddhism* are examples). Hinduism isn't founded, since it has no single founder. A devout Hindu may worship one or several Hindu gods, the most prominent examples including Shiva, Vishnu and Shakti. This lack of orthodoxy – there is no right way to be a Hindu – has been an aspect that has particularly appealed to westerners raised in a prescriptive Christian tradition.

Nevertheless, the beliefs of most Hindus have a few things in common. Among these are the pursuit of the four Puruṣārthas, or proper aims or goals of human existence. These are defined to be Dharma (ethics and duties), Artha (work and prosperity), Kāma (emotions and sexuality) and Moksha (freedom and liberation). How many of these do you have nailed down? It's a common observation that in western societies, we tend to place too much emphasis on love and work, to the exclusion of all else. ('That's all there is,' Sigmund Freud once declared.) But what about Dharma and Moksha, a Hindu might ask. Early western attempts to describe Hindu spirituality emphasised its emotional and childlike aspects. Although this interpretation has been criticised as imperialist, these perceived qualities exerted a strong allure, particularly during the counterculture.

In 1968, The Beatles travelled to India to attend the ashram of the Maharishi Mahesh Yogi. The Hindu guru taught transcendental meditation (TM), by which practitioners would chant a uniquely tailored mantra until they achieved a sense of oneness with the universe. It seems to have worked for John Lennon*. Thanks to TM, he said, 'I'm a better person and I wasn't bad before.' However, he became suspicious when the Maharishi suggested the band should pay a quarter of royalties from their next album into a Swiss bank account for the promotion of TM. 'Over my dead body,' Lennon retorted. The Beatles and their guru fell out, amid claims by the former that he had made sexual overtures to some of his female acolytes, including the actress Mia Farrow. The Maharishi's followers countered that the pop stars had annoyed him by taking LSD*, flouting his ban on drugs. Despite the bickering, the association between The Beatles and the Maharishi helped to make meditation a trendy practice in the west, which it remains to this day.

Buddhism

Siddhartha Gautama, later known as the Buddha, was the original boho. His father, who ruled a kingdom in northern

India around 600 BC, was told that his son would be either a great king or a holy man, depending on whether he saw the suffering of those who lived beyond the palace walls. Preferring that he should be a king, he tried to keep the boy confined, but Gautama slipped away, witnessed the wretchedness of mankind and, to his father's dismay, became a spiritual seeker. He settled himself down under a fig tree (also called the Bodhi Tree, or Bo for short) and refused to leave until he had come up with a way to end all human suffering. His consequent insights were formulated into the philosophical system, sometimes called a religion, known as Buddhism.

Enthusiastic readers of self-help books will have noticed that they like nothing better than to deal in numbered lists. (The Six Key Life Goals. The Nine Defining Qualities of Cool. That sort of thing.) Buddhists began the practice. Seekers after enlightenment learn that they must grapple with the Four Noble Truths (the existence of suffering, what causes it, the key to ending it and the path thereto). They may be required to follow the Eight Precepts, which all take the form of renunciations. The last three are particularly harsh. You must refrain from eating anything after midday. You must refrain from dancing and playing music, wearing jewellery and cosmetics, and attending shows. And thirdly, you must refrain from using high or luxurious seats and bedding.

As something of a niche pursuit in the western world, Buddhism has had a special appeal for anyone seeking an unconventional life. The meditative practitioner will also be austere of dress, emotionally self-controlled, and increasingly laconic. (This 'retreat from words', as George Steiner has noted, is a spiritual process also recommended by the Taoist Lao Tzu*.) The list of those who have explored Buddhism at one time or another includes Jack Kerouac*, Michel Foucault*, David Bowie*, Che Guevara*, J.D. Salinger* and Steve Jobs*. Some say that it isn't a religion since the Buddha was not a god. That's true. But his teachings offer a useful moral code and the dulcet promise of freedom from the fear of death: two defining attractions of any religion.

Christianity

From a European point of view, Christianity began as an eastern religion, whose influence spread west from the Levant. It is now arguably 'uncool' by virtue of being the most popular religion in the world, and for a couple of other reasons we won't go into here. Yet the religion retains one trump card in the cool stakes, namely that its founder, Jesus Christ, is apparently the only man in history to have possessed and professed all of our Nine Defining Qualities of Coolness.

Let's consider them in turn, as they're there to be found in the canonical version of events presented by the Gospels. STYLE and REBELLION: These almost go without saying in the case of Christ. He rebels against the Roman occupation of Judea, the greed of the money-lenders in the temple, and the pedantry of the Jewish elders, and he does so with smart, softly-spoken panache. When the High Priest, Caiaphas, asks him if he is really the son of God, he replies suavely, 'You are the one saying it.' ROOTLESSNESS: He is an itinerant preacher. RECKLESSNESS: Knowing it will result in his death, he pursues his mission to its end. PROMISCUITY/ CELIBACY: Sex isn't important to Christ, a detachment emblematised in the miraculous manner of his birth. SELF-EXPRESSION: Short of making the world, creative self-expression doesn't get much grander than founding your own religion. FLAMBOYANCE/AUSTERITY: Before embarking on his ministry, he spends forty days fasting in the wilderness. TACITURNITY/ELOQUENCE: He communicates his philosophy by sweetly constructed parables. EMOTIONAL SELF-CONTROL: If someone strikes your right cheek, he advises, you should respond by offering them your left.

A dealer in parables, Christ believed fiction could communicate ideas that were truer than the truth. His own story too can be interpreted as a parable, its moral message being one not only of gentleness but also of humility. (His cot was a livestock trough; he was crucified between a pair of common thieves.) Christianity began as an underdog religion, whose flame caught in a state occupied by an imperialist oppressor. Following a classic cool story arc, the underdog triumphed over the overlord, and the religion of the minority became that of the majority.

Accessories

Hats & scarves

In George Gissing's 1886 novel *A Life's Morning*, a character loses his hat when it's blown out of the window of a train. Rather than suffer the shame of walking around bareheaded, he instantly spends the only money he has on buying a replacement. As George Orwell noted, to understand the man's behaviour we would have to imagine somehow losing our trousers on public transport. In Victorian times, that is to say, absolutely everyone wore a hat. This remained the case until the rise of the car in the mid-20th century, after which people walked less, and hats fell out of fashion. That was the moment at which they became cool. Thenceforth, if you wore a hat, you were making a statement, at least part of which was that in matters of style, you went your own way.

Scarves originated in Ancient Rome, where they were worn around the neck or tied at the waist, and used for practical reasons. In cold weather, they kept you warm. In hot, they were used for wiping the sweat from the face, or protecting you from the sun. The first hat with a sun-brim was the *petasos*, which can be seen in Ancient Greek vase paintings being sported by rural types. (Its extreme descendant is the Mexican sombrero.) It's kind of curious, but also convenient, the way that hats and scarves can be worn to protect not only against the sun and heat, but also against the rain and cold. To wear them these days may imply a bohemian level of poverty: owning no car, and unable to afford public transport, you are forced to walk, which exposes you to the elements. In addition, perhaps, you don't have the money to pay for heating or a well-insulated home. Or, just conceivably, you're aiming for a vague air of criminality. Hats and scarves were worn by outlaws in the Old West to hide their faces when pulling a bank heist. In H.G. Wells's 1897 novella *The Invisible Man*, the sinister protagonist pulls his hat down so low, and his scarf up so high, that he successfully disguises the fact that he doesn't have a face at all.

A flamboyant scarf, like a flamboyant hat, may also proclaim your style. In the song 'You're So Vain', Carly Simon describes the narcissist of the title (whom she recently revealed as the actor Warren Beatty) as wearing a scarf the colour of apricot. In practice, both accessories may also serve the useful function of disguising the signs of ageing. An adult holding to an adolescent ideal, the cool individual (certain elderly rock stars spring to mind) may be sensitive about a receding hairline or wrinkled neck. So he caps one and scarfs the other.

Beards

People tend to assume that whatever they've grown up with is the 'natural' way of things, unlikely ever to change. This is a judgement usually made without any reference to nature.

Those born in the west in the second half of the 20th century regard it as 'natural', for example, that the stories of movies should be accompanied by music, when in reality it's no more natural than if every novel came with a specially selected CD to be played while reading it. Similarly, it seems natural to most men to set aside time every morning to slather their faces with cream, which they then scrape off with a sliver of sharpened steel. In reality, of course, what would be far more natural would be not to shave but to sport a large bushy beard.

This naturalness was what appealed to hippies such as Allen Ginsberg*, who grew beards during the 1960s counterculture – this and the fact that, since beards weren't widely worn, wearing one was a declaration that you were rebelling against the norm. Add, too, that when combined with long flowing hair, the look could lend you a Messianic aspect, which might encourage some to regard you as wise (a style adopted at various points by John Lennon* and Steve Jobs*). The Victorians had taken it one step further, favouring a fuller beard, and hair that was slightly less long, conjuring a look of God Himself. It was then that intellectual system-builders such as Charles Darwin, Karl Marx and Sigmund Freud were constructing their alternative structures of thought, which risked supplanting those offered by organised religion. All three would pause at intervals in their work, and stroke thick, God-like beards.

It was a look that also suited empire-builders. If you're going to usurp someone else's country, it helps if you have an air of authority. From 1860 until 1916, all British soldiers were obliged by their terms of service to cultivate a moustache. The rule was phased out during the First World War because facial hair got in the way of gas masks. This, combined with the availability of cheap disposable razors, ushered in the clean-shaven century in which most of us were brought up. Recently, though, beards have enjoyed a resurgence of popularity. The reasons for this are unclear. Perhaps it's that, since the rise of the internet, more people work from home, so can skip the laborious business of shaving. Or is it that our inherited value systems have once more been coming under threat, as they did in the Victorian era? Is each man suggesting by his beard that, in these uncertain times, he, at least, can be relied upon?

Tattoos & piercings

In the early autumn of 1991, two German tourists were walking in the hills on the Austrian–Italian border when they stumbled upon a 5,300-year-old corpse. Preserved in the snow, the man – who was later christened 'Ötzi' because he was found in the Ötztal Alps – was carrying an axe, a flint-bladed knife and a quiver containing fourteen arrows. He was also wearing a bearskin cap with a leather chin strap, had an ear-piercing of 7–11mm in diameter, and displayed 61 tattoos in the form of dark lines on his body. One cannot help wondering if these accessories were conventional at the time, or if Ötzi was some kind of Bronze Age hipster.

The discovery put paid to a long-held belief that the techniques of tattooing had first been introduced to Europe by one Joseph Banks, the naturalist on Captain Cook's expedition to Tahiti in 1769, during which he had witnessed the practice among the Polynesian natives and been so intrigued he had submitted to being tattooed himself. (There is also, incidentally, evidence of tattooing in Ancient Roman times, when the foreheads of slaves who had attempted to escape were marked with a 'K', short for a phrase meaning 'Stop me, I'm a runaway.') What may be true is that Banks's enthusiasm for tattooing helped to make it a trend in the West – especially, at first, among the upper classes. Post-Banks, it became a tradition among sailors to pick up tattoos on their travels, turning their bodies into a map of the past. It was and is a visual demonstration, at the same time, of the willingness to endure the pain of getting the things etched on the skin in the first place.

Piercings, which indicate a similar courage, are another naval custom. As a rite of passage, sailors were given earrings to mark their first crossing of the equator. As with tattoos, the multifarious mythology surrounding the origin of different piercings is often dubious. There's an off-putting story, which is surely untrue, that genital piercing was pioneered by Queen Victoria's consort Prince Albert, to enable him discreetly to pin down his unfeasibly large penis. But we won't dwell on that. In the 16th century it became fashionable in England for men to sport earrings, hence the images of William Shakespeare with a ring in his left ear; ditto King Charles I (also the left ear). As a rule, though, piercings, like tattoos, mark you out as unconventional. Above all, they show a willingness to commit to a decision of style, even if it's one you may later come to regret.

The actor Johnny Depp – a kind of modern-day Ötzi, perhaps – has always been a keen accessoriser. However, he must have rued his decision, while dating the actress Winona Ryder, to tattoo the words 'Winona Forever' on his right arm. After the relationship ended, he felt obliged to have the two letters erased, so it read 'Wino Forever'.

Maxims

'Live fast, die young, and have a good-looking corpse.'

This motto is often wrongly attributed to James Dean*. According to one of his biographers, the movie star was fond of quoting it. Yet it was in common currency long before Dean came along. The first half of the saying, about living fast and dying young, can be traced back to the 19th century. The first instance of the fuller form appears in a report printed in a California newspaper about the divorce proceedings in 1920 between a certain Irene L. Luce and Oscar B. Luce. A letter was quoted in which the liberated woman had told her husband that she couldn't be bothered to remain married to him. 'I intend to live a fast life, die young, and be a beautiful corpse,' she explained.

In 1947 the sentiment appeared as the life motto of Nick Romano, the anti-hero of the bestselling juvenile-delinquency novel *Knock On Any Door* by Willard Motley. Two years later, a film adaptation came out, which used it as the poster tagline: 'He knows all the angles, loves all the girls, hates all cops. His code: Live fast, die young and have a good-looking corpse!' In the movie (which was directed by Nicholas Ray, better remembered for his later film *Rebel Without a Cause* starring James Dean) it was spoken by a preternaturally handsome young actor named John Derek.

Fortunately for Derek, he didn't follow his character's philosophy to the letter in his personal life. If he had died young, he would never have married the Bond girl Ursula Andress, or the *Dynasty* actress Linda Evans, or, for that matter, a girl 30 years his junior named Mary Cathleen Collins, who was destined to become better known to the public as the model and actress Bo Derek.

Decades later, the career cool-chaser Quentin Tarantino* would wield a version of the line in his screenplay for the film *True Romance*, in which the protagonist rhapsodises about the coolness of Elvis Presley*, who in the film *Jailhouse Rock* didn't care about anything except 'living fast, dying young and leaving a good-looking corpse'. An even more enjoyable usage is the variation offered by Ricky Gervais in the TV show *The Office* (2001). He's committed to the ideal of living fast, he says, but he's not so sure about dying young. On balance, he would prefer to die old. He presents this as proof that he doesn't play by 'the rules'.

'Work like you don't need the money, love like you've never been hurt, and dance like no one's watching.'
It's a terrific line, which the rock star Bono* likes to quote in interviews from time to time. But who was the first person to say it? As with the exhortation to 'Live fast, die young, and have a good-looking corpse', the authorship has been disputed. It has been attributed to Mark Twain and the baseball pitcher Satchel Paige, among others.

The first thing to note about this saying, though, is how closely it maps onto some of our defining cool qualities, specifically those of recklessness, promiscuity and self-expression. And how neatly it summarises the cool attitude towards time: the first part seems to dispense with concerns for the future, while the second dismisses thoughts of the past, and the third advises such absolute immersion in the present, it's as if other people actually cease to exist.

It's tempting to think that the line might be one that was never definitively invented by anyone, but one of those anonymous sayings honed to perfection by being repeated over the decades until it reached its current unimprovable form, like 'Be kind, for everyone you meet is fighting a hard battle' (often falsely attributed to Plato) or 'The key to seduction is to make the other person feel attractive' (ditto Le Duc de la Rochefoucauld). But no. The truth is, it originated in a country song called 'Come From the Heart', which was first recorded by the singer Guy Clark in 1987. 'I have seen it attributed to everyone from an unnamed Buddhist* monk to the great Satchel Paige, but it just isn't so,' says one of the song's co-authors, Richard Leigh. 'I think the folks out there must be unconsciously disappointed that something that cool came from such ordinary people.'

Guys who had it but blew it

Ernest Hemingway

Ernest Hemingway's enormous literary achievements when young, and his later decline into bloated self-parody, were triggered by accidents. The first was while the American author, who was then unpublished, was living with his wife Hadley in Paris in the 1920s. She lost a suitcase containing all his fiction up to that point, along with his carbon copies. Devastated, Hemingway never forgave her. In hindsight, though, it may have done him a favour, getting rid of his rough-hewn early efforts, so that when his first books were published, they launched his revolutionary adult style fully formed: the simple, seemingly detached journalistic sentences that quietly accumulated a powerful emotional charge.

In Our Time (1925). *The Sun Also Rises* (1926). *Men Without Women* (1927). *A Farewell to Arms* (1929). In those first few works, Hemingway not only pioneered a new way of writing, which restricted itself almost entirely to physical description as a way to evoke emotions. He also created a new kind of protagonist. The Hemingway hero was physically fit, softly spoken, thoughtful but not cerebral, irreligious but spiritual, a drinker but not a drunkard, a lover of women but not a ladies' man, prone to occasional losses of temper, essentially kind. By all accounts, it was a version (albeit an idealised one) of the young Hemingway himself. Yet his youthful persona, like the influential prose style in which he presented it, proved tough to sustain. In 1928, the same year as he was writing *A Farewell to Arms*, Hemingway came home from a hard night's drinking and sat down on the lavatory. When he tried to pull the chain, he accidentally grabbed a cord attached to the skylight, and yanked the whole thing down on his head. It was one of a series of injuries that eventually reduced the author to a physical wreck, barely able to write at all, let alone write well.

The self-importance of *Death in the Afternoon* (1932) was an early sign of the decline to come. *To Have and Have Not* (1937) was plain bad. *Across the River and Into the Trees* (1950) is actually unreadable. Worse even than his literary crimes, though, was the terrible bearded bore and alcoholic braggart that Hemingway became, a deterioration all the more painful for how brilliant he had been. There's an excruciating late letter in which he boasts to someone about how well he has just 'f***ed' his wife. And he openly declared himself a better writer than Turgenev and Maupassant, and the equal of Stendhal. It's possible he was joking. Orson Welles once said that only those who knew Hemingway personally knew how incredibly funny he could be. So yes, maybe Hemingway was joking. We'll have to hope that he was.

Robert De Niro

What happened to Robert De Niro? In the 1970s he was hailed as the greatest actor of his generation, the new Marlon Brando*. That decade is studded with his edgy, vital, virtuosic performances, from his driven, never daunted Vito Corleone in *The Godfather, Part II* to his haunted, hard-as-nails Vietnam veteran in *The Deer Hunter*. His neurotic, psychotic Travis Bickle in *Taxi Driver*. His tragicomic portrayal of the boxer Jake LaMotta in *Raging Bull*. From these heights of intensity, De Niro has descended to slapstick and slack self-parody in (I'm sorry but) third-rate gross-out comedies.

In his heyday, the man was known for taking his Method* training to extremes, particularly in his preparation for roles. He spent weeks driving a taxi before playing Bickle, and put on 60lb by gorging on pasta and ice cream in order to play the gone-to-seed LaMotta in the latter stages of *Raging Bull*. That can't have been all that much fun and perhaps that's why he reached a point where he said to himself: I just don't want to do this kind of thing any more. It's hard to be sure, since De Niro has tended to avoid interviews and usually seemed deliberately bland in the rare ones he's given. Conceivably, he reached a turning point in 1981 when John Hinckley, after attempting to assassinate President Reagan, said afterwards that he'd been inspired by *Taxi Driver* (he seemed to think that he *was* Travis Bickle). Or the change may have come after the death from a drug overdose of De Niro's close friend, the maverick comedian John Belushi.

What we do know is that the 1980s was a bit of a hit-and-miss decade for the actor. The 1990s was more miss than hit (remember *Mary Shelley's Frankenstein*?). Since then, it has been mainly misses. The titles of *Righteous Kill* and *Dirty Grandpa* give a sense of the quality of their contents. We shouldn't hit our heroes, but in De Niro's case it's hard to resist. I suppose we just miss him.

On the road

Cars

In the 5th century BC tragedy *Hippolytus*, the sleek Greek hero prefers to race his chariot than consort with the opposite sex, and is punished for his arrogance when his horses run amok. In a film adaptation released in 1962, the story was brought up to date. The chariot was replaced by a 1960 Aston Martin DB4 MkII, which puts paid to the protagonist when he swerves off a snaky coastal road to avoid an oncoming truck. Fast cars were to mid-20th century man, in other words, what hunting and chariot racing had been to the Greek: a fairground ride for one, a way to display your manliness, and a demonstration to women that you had interests other than them – although, if they were feeling lucky, there was room for one passenger.

This ambivalent connection between cars and sex – implying both rejection and solicitation – was first forged in the US in the 1950s, when the number of automobiles doubled. For the first time, the American teenager could escape the prescriptive gaze of parents, whether to make out at the drive-in, or flaunt a devil-may-care attitude by driving dangerously fast, or both. It was a cultural shift enacted in the movie *Rebel Without a Cause*, in which James Dean* and a well-built rival named Buzz engage in a macho game of 'chickie' that involves driving stolen cars towards a cliff-edge, to see who will lose his nerve first and bail. Somewhat implausibly, Buzz gets his sleeve caught on the door handle and plunges to his doom, giving Dean cause to furrow his brow and brood upon life's mysteries. In real life, the actor was a car fanatic who raced in contests until his premature death at the wheel of his Porsche 550 Spyder.

Other cars that have played an important role in cool's history: the 1949 Hudson Commodore, which transports the principal characters across America in Jack Kerouac's* novel *On the Road*; the 1963 Aston Martin DB5 put through its paces by James Bond* in *Goldfinger* and subsequent movies; the 1968 Ford Mustang driven by Steve McQueen in the film *Bullitt* in what is still considered the greatest car chase of any movie. In more recent years, the perceived coolness of automobiles has been somewhat eroded by environmental concerns. The burning of fuel and churning up of the track, which once signalled mastery, now suggests immodesty, and the passion for top gear has come to seem a little retro and right-wing: the kind of occupation that might begin as an innocent hobby and end with you punching someone in the face for bringing you a plate of cold meat when you were hoping for a steak.

Motorbikes

Movies about motorbikes marked the beginning and the end – or at least, the beginning of the end – of the era of classic cool. First came Marlon Brando* as Johnny Strabler, the leader of a leather-clad biker gang in *The Wild One*, which kick-started the whole business when it was released in 1953, and whose influence, as the saying goes, cannot be overstated. There's a theory that The Beatles may have borrowed their name from The Beetles, the rival gang in the movie. Elvis Presley* is said to have based the style of his character in the film *Jailhouse Rock* on Johnny. After seeing *The Wild One*, James Dean* went straight out and bought himself a Triumph motorbike in emulation of Brando's 1950 Triumph Thunderbird 6T.

The film that flagged up the demise of classic cool was *Easy Rider**, which reached the screen sixteen years later in 1969. Its star, Peter Fonda, had conceived his cool-biker persona a few years earlier in another biker movie, *The Wild Angels*, whose tag line read, 'Their credo is violence … Their God is hate …' Yet in *Easy Rider* his character doesn't want any trouble. The film features several scenes of Fonda and Dennis Hopper just cruising along on their low-slung, elongated Harley Davidson choppers, their expressions suggesting a relaxed delight in the freedom offered by the vast spaces of the American interior. The word 'chopper', incidentally, means a bike that has been 'chopped', which is to say modified. The ones used in *Easy Rider* had indeed been specially designed for it. In fact, to achieve the right look, they had minimal padding on the seats, making them extremely uncomfortable to ride. By the end of each day's filming, the actors could barely move. The film should have been called *Uneasy Rider*.

Motorbikes are self-evident symbols of freedom, even more than cars since the cool rider isn't encased within a metal shell. They are correspondingly more dangerous and correspondingly more cool. Statistics show that, per mile travelled, you are 37 times more likely to suffer a fatal accident while on a motorbike, compared with when driving a car. Motorbikes are also less vulnerable than cars to the charge of environmental irresponsibility, since – notwithstanding the fact that when they were invented in the late 19th century, they were originally dubbed 'petrol cycles' – they consume relatively little fuel by comparison.

Drugs

Marijuana

Effects. Smoking dope or marijuana – which is made from the dried flowers, leaves and stems of the cannabis plant – is relaxing. Users lose their shyness, feel 'high', and then peaceful. It can also, in my experience, reduce otherwise quite serious people to helpless fits of giggling followed by a sudden dash to the lavatory to throw up. There's a tendency, too, to overrate the profundity of the philosophical insights glimpsed while high on marijuana. There's a nice example of this in the 1978 movie *Animal House* in which a hip professor played by Donald Sutherland shares a joint with his wide-eyed students. One of them (Tom Hulce) is struck by the realisation that the universe could be a tiny atom in the fingernail of a giant – which further means (his pupils dilate with excitement) that a tiny atom in his own fingernail could conceivably contain an entire universe.

History. Unlike LSD and heroin, which are synthesised by chemists, marijuana is a naturally occurring herb that has been used as a stimulant for thousands of years. In some cultures it has been an entheogen, meaning it was thought to facilitate the path to a higher state of spiritual awareness (but see above for what might be termed 'the Hulce effect'). Many artists and authors say that smoking marijuana has helped to shake them free of conventional ways of thinking and released them from the inhibitions that constrict their creativity. There's even a theory, which is not widely accepted by scholars, that William Shakespeare may have been a smoker, based on his reference to the 'noted weed' in Sonnet 76.

Risks. In a report published in the *British Medical Journal* in 2011, marijuana was rated the least harmful of nineteen stimulants including LSD, heroin and alcohol. Some researchers have argued that it may trigger schizophrenia, and that it can exacerbate paranoia in those already prone to it. One of my friends, who was normally outgoing and jolly, always became introverted and irritable after smoking a joint. I remember another, in his teens, announcing that he basically didn't want to do anything in his life except smoke dope and get high. He is now a solicitor.

LSD

Effects. An LSD experience is known as 'a trip' because it takes a while and transports you to places you don't normally visit. Lysergic acid diethylamide, also known as acid, is typically ingested in the form of a blotting paper tab swallowed or held under the tongue until it dissolves. The effects kick in after an hour or so and may last as long as twelve. Their most striking feature is hallucinatory. Surroundings mutate, colours seem unnaturally bright (sunglasses may be advisable), and there's a distortion of time and space. Aficionados believe the world as perceived during an acid trip is as real as, and possibly realer than, that presented by the conventional perception of a sober mind.

History. The stimulant was first created by the Swiss chemist Albert Hofmann in 1938, but it wasn't until five years later that, to his immense surprise, he discovered its hallucinogenic powers. In the 1960s and 70s, it became the coolest drug in town because its effects were so bizarre. Its urgent advocates included the novelists Aldous Huxley and Ken Kesey, and the mischievous Harvard psychology professor Timothy Leary*, who encouraged Americans to 'turn on, tune in and drop out'. By this he meant that he believed the world would be a nicer, happier place if everyone did LSD. People would understand that many of their dearest assumptions and deepest concerns were the result of cultural and cognitive conditioning. The aim was to see beyond these limits: a mission Kesey summarised by his decision to give the name 'Further' to the bus in which he travelled around America, preaching the benefits of LSD. The rock band The Doors took their name from Huxley's book *The Doors of Perception*, in which he had described his experiences with the hallucinogen mescaline. He had himself borrowed the title from a line in a poem by William Blake*: 'If the doors of perception were cleansed, everything would appear to man as it is: infinite.'

Risks. Generally speaking, the worst danger of taking LSD is suffering what is known as a 'bad trip', which can be terrifying. According to Leary, the danger of this happening can be minimised if the 'set' and 'setting' are right, which is to say that the user should have a calm mindset at the start of the experience, and the chosen location should be peaceful. There is also a risk of flashbacks, whereby users will later relive the effects of a trip but without taking the drug again. Nevertheless, LSD is non-addictive and rated relatively low in terms of attendant risks.

Heroin

Effects. Injecting heroin gives the user a massive rush of euphoria, followed by a feeling of extreme relaxation, oblivious to pain and detached from the worries of the world.

History. The chemical diamorphine, which is more commonly known as heroin, was first synthesised from the opium poppy by the German chemist Felix Hoffmann in the late 19th century. The head of Bayer, the pharmaceutical company he worked for, gave it the name Heroin after the German word *heroisch* meaning heroic or strong, because that was how it made you feel. From 1898 it was available over the counter in high-street chemists, where it was actually marketed as 'Heroin', and promoted as a painkiller and, believe it or not, cough suppressant. That's right. Suffering from a tickle in the back of the throat? Try Heroin. With the passing years, the drug's dangers became apparent. It was banned in the US in 1924, with Europe soon following suit.

Risks. In research published in the *British Medical Journal*, heroin topped the list of nineteen stimulants for the level of risk it poses to users. Proverbially addictive, it requires increased concentrations of dosage to achieve the desired rush. This, combined with the fact that it's hard to be certain of the purity or intensity of the heroin you've acquired, is what can lead to disaster. One of the most common causes of death is asphyxiation resulting from the way heroin slows down the function of the lungs to the point at which a user may cease to breathe altogether. Alternatively a heroin death may be caused by asphyxiation due to vomiting. The more squalid aspects of addiction are dramatised by the film *Trainspotting* and described by William S. Burroughs'* first-hand account in his 1953 book *Junkie*. Repeated injection of the drug into the main veins of the arm may cause them to collapse, leaving the user forced to resort to more obscure channels, such as the femoral vein in the groin.

Crazy s***

Conspiracy theories

In the 1969 film *Easy Rider**, while smoking his first joint, a character named George, played by Jack Nicholson, gets a little carried away. He explains that ever since man 'started bouncing radar beams off the moon', aliens have been 'living and working' among us. The government knows about it, but doesn't admit it because of the shock it would cause to 'our antiquated systems'. Another of the characters, with a smile, asks, 'How's your joint, George?' What the scene implies is that there may, just possibly, be a link between the propensity to believe in conspiracy theories and the mood of paranoia and free-associative thinking (the having of the thought is tantamount to proof of its validity) that can be engendered by being off your head on marijuana*.

As the phrase implies, a conspiracy theory is usually a negative hypothesis (evil forces are conspiring) which explains a negative phenomenon, such as the 9/11 attacks or the wealth gap. It's a psychic mechanism that is designed to ease psychic distress in three ways. Firstly, it offers to make sense of something that seems dismayingly senseless. Secondly, the explanation tends to be pleasingly simple (it's *all* because of such and such). And thirdly, any such theory is attractive to the conspiracy theorist – sometimes referred to as a 'conspiracist' – because it suggests they have specialist knowledge. They are, in other words, part of an in-crowd, because they understand what the cloth-headed majority doesn't. And that, naturally, makes them kind of cool.

Given these links between coolness and conspiracism, it's hardly surprising that the energetic theorist will come up with almost any hypothesis to ease the psychic distress caused by the death of their cool role models. Kurt Cobain* and Albert Camus*, so we're told, were both murdered (the latter by the KGB). Elvis Presley* faked his death to boost flagging record sales. Amelia Earhart* did likewise because she was on a secret mission for the US government. Hunter S. Thompson* was dispatched because he was about to reveal that the destruction of the World Trade Center was caused not by planes crashing into it but by explosions detonated within the building. All of which, with the best will in the world, tends to prompt the response: how's your joint, George?

Black magic

There's a memorable moment in the autobiography of the Rolling Stones guitarist Keith Richards*, when he describes how a certain Stanislas Klossowski de Rola (the son of the painter Balthus) used his professed knowledge of black magic as an aid to seduction. The louche aristocrat had 'the bullshit credentials of the period', Richards notes, with perhaps a touch of envy, 'the patter of mysticism, the lofty talk of alchemy and the secret arts, all basically employed in the service of leg-over'. Which leaves one wondering if this has always been part of the allure of the occult.

In literature, black, which is to say malign, magic (as opposed to benign white magic) has always lent a certain sinister glamour. One thinks of the beautiful witch Circe in Homer's* *Odyssey*, who uses her drugs to turn the hero's companions into swine, of Faust and Prospero, or more recently the figures of Sauron and Voldemort in the *Lord of the Rings* and *Harry Potter* stories. Yet it's not only in fiction that the dark arts impress. In a 2002 poll, the occultist Aleister Crowley, once dubbed by the press 'the wickedest man in the world', was voted the 73rd 'Greatest Briton' in history. Despite his obvious charlatanry, sexual deviance and general unpleasantness (which prompted his mother, who might have been expected to be partial, to nickname him 'The Beast'), Crowley is apparently revered for his insights into arcane and devious wizardry: especially his explorations of alchemy (turning base metals to gold), astrology (predicting the future according to the alignment of the stars) and the nefarious, hilarious area of occult expertise known as 'sex magic'.

Sex magic – a notion that makes me giggle every time I think about it – has been taken extremely seriously by occultists throughout history. There was, for instance, a 19th-century specialist from New York named Paschal Beverly Randolph, who claimed you could achieve anything you wanted (power, wealth) simply by thinking about it really hard while having great sex. But the sex had to be *really great*,

Randolph stressed. It had to involve a 'superior woman', with what he called 'perfect sexive and orgasmal ability'. Well, he would say that, wouldn't he?

Then there was the smouldering Russian mystic Maria de Naglowska, who believed best results could be achieved by 'erotic ritual hanging'. We'll just have to take her word for that one.

Insanity

Mental illness is not a joke. Believe me. So why is it that, in its milder forms, it carries the aureate glow of cool? Anyone who doubts this need only think of the cinematic careers of Dennis Hopper and Jack Nicholson to come up with dozens of illustrative instances. The mildest form of all is feigned madness – which you might say isn't madness at all, if it weren't for the argument that you'd have to be mad to want to feign it. Hamlet*, for example, adopts an 'antic disposition', so his uncle Claudius will underestimate him while he finds a way to test if he murdered his father. Yet scholars have devoted careers to discussing whether Hamlet may actually be mad in any case, and that he adopts his stratagem of feigning it partly because he was already headed in that direction.

In Ken Kesey's 1962 novel *One Flew Over the Cuckoo's Nest*, the protagonist Randle McMurphy (played by Jack Nicholson in the movie version) pretends to be mad so that, instead of prison, he'll get what he hopes will be the cushier deal of serving time in a mental institution. Insisting on treating his fellow inmates as human beings, he inspires them to rebellion, and ends up being reduced to a vegetative state by the twin punitive 'treatments' of lobotomy and electroconvulsive therapy.

Kesey's beautiful, disturbing book was in the vanguard of what became known as the anti-psychiatry movement. In the sphere of academia, some of its arguments were expressed by Michel Foucault's* *Madness and Civilisation*, which critiqued the peculiar brutality of contemporary treatments for perceived mental abnormality. In *The Divided Mind*, the Scottish psychologist R.D. Laing suggested the diagnosis of schizophrenia was delivered with a false air of authority. In reality, he said, the condition was 'a theory, not a fact'. In a lecture series published posthumously, Foucault further suggested that the figure regarded by society as insane (an example he gives is the court jester) may serve a useful social function. He or she is a licensed *parrhesiastes*: a word that literally signifies one who says everything, although in this context it means the person who says the unsayable. And that, just occasionally, is the thing that most needs to be said.

Cool movies

The Magnificent Seven

One reason why *The Magnificent Seven* (1960) is the second most shown movie on US television (the first is *The Wizard of Oz*) is that it provides a masterclass in cool. The seven gunslingers of the title, who team up against a gang of bandits terrorising a Mexican village, represent seven distinct but significant cool types. There's Yul Brynner as the existential man in black; Steve McQueen the easy-going gambler; Brad Dexter the amoral opportunist; Charles Bronson the silent strongman; James Coburn the stoic virtuoso; Robert Vaughn the angst-ridden dandy; and last but not least, the young actor Horst Buchholz, sometimes known as the German James Dean*, who represents the juvenile delinquent type.

Considered now, the cast seems a dream team, but only Brynner was a Hollywood star at the time, while the rest had mainly worked in television. Aware of this, they tried to steal scenes by improvising attention-grabbing tics and tricks once the cameras were rolling. McQueen was so competitive that Brynner finally told him if he didn't cut it out, he would take his hat off in every scene in which they both appeared, revealing his shaven head. No one then would be looking at McQueen. McQueen cooled it and his performance is cooler as a result.

Although Coburn and McQueen both run him a close

second on the coolness front, it's Brynner's movie. No explanation is given for why an articulate bald-headed Russian would be working as a cowboy* and gun-for-hire, or why he would choose to dress from head to toe in black in scorching temperatures. He is simply there, passing through. Asked where he's come from, he jerks a thumb over his shoulder; asked where he's going, he points an index finger ahead of him. It's all tremendously camp, as is the swing-hippy way he walks, which may just be what happens to you if you spend too much time on horseback. But the emphasis is on the word tremendous. Brynner embodies the classic existentialist cowboy, a kind of Camus* with six-shooters. With his dying breath, the villain Calvera asks why a man like him would risk his life for a bunch of Mexican peasants. Cool as ever, Brynner doesn't answer.

Easy Rider

By rights, the 1969 movie Easy Rider should have been a disaster. It was made on a tiny budget, directed by a first-time director – the actor Dennis Hopper – and for much of the time while he was shooting it, most of the cast and crew seem to have been off their heads on drugs. The first cut that Hopper came up with was around four hours long. He had to be distracted while someone else was brought in to edit it down to a more palatable 95 minutes. Yet inexplicably, by some mad strand of movie alchemy, the final product turned out to be one of the coolest films ever made.

After selling some drugs in California, a pair of bikers, Billy (Hopper, paranoid and moustachioed) and Wyatt (a laid-back Peter Fonda wearing a motorcycle helmet emblazoned with the American flag) set off on a road trip on their big-swinging Harley Davidson choppers. Their picturesque and picaresque adventures include falling in with a hippy commune, hanging out with a 'square' but entertaining lawyer (Jack Nicholson), and getting beaten up by rednecks. Reaching New Orleans, they pick up a couple of sympathetic prostitutes and enjoy the Mardi Gras festival in a psychedelic, acid-fuelled haze. 'We did it!' Hopper declares triumphantly. Fonda disagrees. 'We blew it,' he replies, speaking for his generation. Shortly afterwards, they are killed by two rednecks.

The symbols are simple. The film is a metaphor for the war between freedom and the fear it can inspire. At one point, Nicholson warns that in the south, hippies have to be careful that they don't get an enforced haircut from conservative locals, which will leave them looking 'like Yul Brynner'. The protagonists' names, Wyatt and Billy, also call up the ghosts of Hollywood gunslingers who pioneered the idea of cool. *Easy Rider* is their swan song. Its melancholy beauty, and devastating ending, signposted the end of the idealism of the 1960s, ushering in the paranoia and protests of the decade that followed, an era when it was no longer about having a good time. You had to get involved, because everything was going to hell, and the living, and the riding, were no longer easy. It was the death of cool, after which there could only be posthumous, postmodernist* comment.

Pulp Fiction

Every now and then, someone creates a work of art that is actually perfect. *Hamlet** isn't perfect. There are a couple too many soliloquies and it's a little on the long side. *The Importance of Being Earnest is* perfect, Oscar Wilde finally admitting he has nothing especially serious to say and saying it perfectly. *Pulp Fiction* is perfect. Seriously. And seriously cool.

When Quentin Tarantino* sat down to write it in a hotel room in Amsterdam in 1992, he seems to have been working on the premise that a perfect movie is an unbroken sequence of seriously cool scenes. Remember the dance in Jack Rabbit Slim's restaurant, when John Travolta, overweight and seedy-looking, reminds us he can move? Or the moment Samuel L. Jackson's gun-toting gangster* slurps the Sprite of his terrified victim, keeping his eyes fixed upon him? Or when Travolta has to slam a needle-full of adrenaline into Uma Thurman's heart after she has overdosed on heroin*, which causes her to jerk upright, like a vampire* awaking from the dead? From musical-romance, to thriller, to horror, in the space of a single movie. Then consider the moment when Bruce Willis's washed-up boxer, about to exact vengeance on a pair of perverted sadists, selects his weapon. First he spies a knife; then he spots a baseball bat. The latter seems to appeal. Then he notices a chainsaw. *Now we're talking*. He's about to set to work when his eye is caught by a shimmering samurai sword on the wall. This scene, some say, shows the director riffling through his movie genres, wondering which to go with next.

Rebellious in their emotionless violence. Reckless in their glamorisation of drug-taking. Stylistically promiscuous. Purely stylish. Tarantino's films – *Pulp Fiction* in particular – sometimes seem like a kind of jukebox of coolness, set to random play. They have so little of substance to say that his more passionate fans feel forced to invest them with a meaning that isn't there. When Travolta opens the briefcase he has retrieved for his boss Marsellus Wallace, using the code 666 (significantly, some say), the contents light up his face with a strange golden glow, but we never get a glimpse of what's inside. There's a crackpot theory that the briefcase contains Wallace's soul. But consider, as an alternative, that the briefcase is empty. Or the point is that it might be. We don't know – and while we don't know what they are, the contents of Tarantino's briefcase, like the cinema screen, give off a perfect glow.

The ride & the fall

Surfing, skateboarding & snowboarding

Surfing came first. The practice of cruising shorewards on the face of a breaking wave was developed by natives in the south and central Pacific. It was brought to California in 1907 by George Freeth, a half-Hawaiian paid by hotelier Henry Huntington to attract tourists by performing, billed as 'the man who walks on water', in front of his hotel on Redondo Beach. So surfing began as a Jesus trick, and its sculpted, long-haired devotees retain a Messianic fervour for their pastime.

It stirred such strong passions that serious fans didn't know what to do with themselves when the sea was flat. To combat their ennui, in the 1940s some strapped roller-skates under boards to create what was originally called 'sidewalk surfing', which actually sounds cooler than the name by which it later became known, which was skate-boarding. This was more democratic than surfing, since the board was less expensive, and you didn't have to inhabit prime real estate beside the sea. On the downside, tarmac hurt if you fell. As a result, skateboarders took to sporting helmets and knee and elbow pads, which was sensible but could feel constricting, and arguably made them look less cool than surfer dudes.

The third in the triumvirate, snowboarding, got off to a weak start. It was initially known as 'snurfing' after being invented in the 1960s by an engineer in Michigan named Sherman Poppen. He strapped two skis together as a device to entertain his daughters, and presumably because it was simpler than teaching them to ski. This is one advantage of snowboarding: it's relatively easy to pick up. You can achieve a decent competence in a day if you're coordinated and the snow's soft enough to fall without losing enthusiasm. Snowboarders divide their pastime into freeriding (snowboarding off-piste), freestyling (doing tricks), and freecarving (snowboarding fast on-piste). The freest kind of snowboarding is the first, which allows you (unlike surfing) to go where you want, and (unlike skateboarding) to commune with nature.

To try to rate these three pastimes is futile, of course. It's a matter of taste. We're on safer ground if we emphasise what they have in common, which is that the aficionados of each have a deep conviction of their own coolness, which they secure with competitively high-tech equipment, and exclusive vocabularies of cool-sounding jargon.

Sky diving, bungee jumping & base jumping

You can, if you want, arrange for someone to shoot you out of a cannon. Or alternatively you could get your kicks from sky diving, bungee jumping or base jumping. The first of these pastimes was developed for sound military reasons as an effective way to transport troops into enemy territory. Yet even sky diving has its infantile aspects. There's a sub-set of practitioners who like to indulge in what's known as 'zoo jumping'. A group of divers leap from a plane, along with some surreal object such as a bicycle, a vacuum cleaner or a car. They then mess about with it during the fall before releasing their parachutes so they're well clear when it smashes into the ground. After landing, a tradition called 'swoop and chug' will sometimes see an accomplice run forward with pints of foaming beer, for the sky divers to knock back in celebration of their accomplishment.

As with the game of poker*, say, the macho air is signalled by popular sayings bandied by free-fallers. 'There are old jumpers and there are bold jumpers, but there are no old, bold jumpers' is an example, which points to the real risk of death. Both aspects – the machismo and the danger of fatality – also attach to the associated sport of bungee jumping. A traditional form known as land diving, using vines rather than bungee cords, is practised as a rite of passage by young males on the Pacific island of Vanuatu. The modern variant was pioneered by David Kirke and Simon Keeling of the Oxford University Dangerous Sports Club, who leapt from the Clifton Suspension Bridge in Bristol in 1979, descended to the length of their cords, and were then jerked back up again, before commencing the undignified up-and-down motion that concludes any bungee jump.

Base jumping is the crazy cousin of the family. The phrase was coined as an acronym: 'base' stands for buildings, antennae, spans (meaning bridges) and earth (meaning cliffs), these being the four platforms from which the jumper embarks. One can't help wondering how many jumps, in practice, are made from antennae, and whether this was simply included to provide a handy vowel. The risk of fatality is far greater than in sky diving because of the proximity to solid structures and also, oddly, because you don't have time to pick up as much speed: at slower speeds, it's harder to control one's trajectory. It's no joke, base jumping. When I chatted to one of its aficionados, he told me a base jumper gets killed roughly once a week. Why, then, do they do it? This seems to be the wrong question. Base jumpers refer scathingly to sceptics as 'wuffos': an abbreviation of 'what do you do that for?' In all three cases, of course, there is an existential rationale. The adrenaline rush comes partly from confronting the fear of death. And that, no doubt, can feel pretty cool.

PART THREE:
THE REAL DEAL

- Courage
- Tenacity
- Kindness
- Mystique
- Eccentricity
- Physicality
- A capacity for solitude
- The lack of self-consciousness
- Indifference to fame and reputation

I didn't know that these qualities were important to me until I had compiled this Real Deal section, which consists of the 25 coolest things on the planet, *in my opinion*. It was only afterwards that I was able to read back through my entries and pick out some common themes. You might call them the NINE REFINING QUALITIES OF COOL, for comparison with our Nine Defining Qualities.

In this section I'm abandoning my mask of objectivity. There's a scene in *The Godfather* when Michael Corleone describes his decision to avenge an attempt on his father's life as not 'personal' but 'strictly business'. This section is the opposite. It's strictly personal.

Homer

Homer is a poet about whom nothing is known. That's a relatively new discovery. For centuries, it was thought that the epic poems *The Iliad* (about the Trojan War) and *The Odyssey* (about the decade-long struggle of the hero Odysseus to return from that war) were the work of a blind, male, wandering bard. Then it was recognised that they bore the hallmarks of oral poems, meaning ones that weren't written down but recited from memory. That is, they were probably created not by one man, but by a series of performance poets over several generations. This makes them not less but more interesting. It seems likely they were edited in response to comments from contemporary audience members. Popular bits remained and got extended; bad or boring bits would be excised. In a sense, you could say that the poems were composed by the Greek people. The experience of reading them is like peering into the mind of Ancient Greece.

Whether or not we accept that this process constitutes an example of 'emergent creativity' (comparable to the way Wikipedia entries evolve), the results are phenomenal: two entirely different but unforgettable story types, dominated by two entirely different but unforgettable heroes. In *The Iliad*, it's Achilles, the warrior who won't fight. He's sulking because his commander-in-chief stole some of his booty, including a hot slave girl named Briseis. As a consequence, the Trojan War tilts in favour of the Trojans, while the Greeks flounder, until something happens that goads Achilles to rejoin the fray. And when he does, his destructive power is awesome.

The Odyssey is more varied, describing the adventures of Odysseus (a quick-witted explorer as well as a fighter), including his encounters with the man-eating Cyclops, the irresistible Sirens, the complacent Lotus Eaters, and all the rest. There are moments of fine poetic delicacy, such as when the hero, shipwrecked and exhausted, crawls ashore on a beach and takes shelter under a bush, and is compared to a spark of fire. And speeches whose resonance hasn't faded, as, for instance, when Odysseus declares that there is nothing finer than true love between a man and woman, which is a source of great delight to their friends, and great annoyance to their enemies.

Hedy Lamarr

Try to think of a handful of people who have excelled in two entirely unconnected fields. A prime minister with his own boutique fashion line, say. Or perhaps an NBA championship-winning basketball player who was also a chess grandmaster. It isn't easy to compile a convincing catalogue, but one who should undoubtedly appear on any such list is the Hollywood sex symbol Hedy Lamarr, who took time out from playing smouldering femmes fatales to invent an unjammable missile-guidance system for use by the Allies in the Second World War.

Born Hedwig Kiesler in Vienna, she rose to fame at the age of eighteen when she became the first actress to portray an orgasm onscreen. For anyone interested, the exuberant and oddly touching scene, which appeared in the 1933 movie *Ekstase*, can be found on YouTube. Soon afterwards, she married a jealous munitions manufacturer named Friedrich Mandl who tried to destroy every copy of the film. Marital life could be tense, with Hedy expected to play the dutiful wife while her husband had the likes of Hitler and Mussolini to dinner at his schloss. It was while listening to his conversations that the girl, who had always been scientifically minded, first developed a serious interest in weapons technology. Yet the shared enthusiasm wasn't enough to save the marriage. In the late 1930s, she did a runner, making her way to Hollywood where, performing as Hedy Lamarr, she became a huge star.

Billed as 'the most beautiful woman in the world', she was dazzling to look at, with perfect bow lips, a delicate nose, and knowing eyes. Few, though, would claim she was a brilliant actress. In any case, she was bored by the boozing and the schmoozing required to sustain her career. In her spare time, Hedy liked nothing better than to hunker over her drafting table and invent things. (Her devices included a traffic light and a tablet for creating a carbonated drink.) In 1940, working with the avant-garde composer George Antheil, she came up with a 'spread spectrum' system for directing torpedoes. Because it continually altered the frequency of the radio waves it used, no one could block it. The US Defense Department didn't adopt the new technology at the time, but dug it out in the 1960s. A version of Hedy's system is now used in all wireless communication, including mobile phones and wifi. It wasn't until decades later that the former film star began to receive the credit for her work. When a communications company gave her an award in the 1990s, she observed drily, 'It's about time.'

The Independent Principality of Sealand

Seven miles off the east coast of England, there is a country. It isn't a very big country. To be precise, it's the smallest country in the world, with a surface area that extends to no more than 6,000 square feet, which is about twice the size of a tennis court. You won't find it on Google Maps and it isn't a member of Nato or the EU. But I know it exists, because I've been there. The full name of this obscure speck of territory is the Independent Principality of Sealand and it has a history that is about as rock 'n' roll as could be imagined.

During the Second World War, the Navy built a handful of fortresses in the North Sea and kitted them out with anti-aircraft guns. They were later abandoned and left to rust away, pounded by the wind and waves. In the 1960s, some were commandeered by so-called radio 'pirates', who used them to broadcast rock music to the nation's teenagers, while making money from advertising. (Commercial radio stations were then banned in the UK, but the forts were outside jurisdiction.) When the British government outlawed the practice, the Bates family from Essex hung on to their fort, which was called Roughs Tower. They rechristened it Sealand and on Christmas Day 1967 they proclaimed it an independent nation.

The Bates family remains in possession of Sealand to this day. The authorities haven't intervened, at least partly because it isn't so easy to launch a maritime operation to retake a military structure that is defended by armed occupants. The Bateses are a pugnacious lot. They have a sense of humour, too. They've designed a flag, coins, stamps and passports for their fledgling country, and the head of the family – first Major Roy Bates; now his son Michael – styles himself 'Prince'. In 1987, when the Territorial Sea Act extended the reach of British territorial waters from three miles to twelve (meaning Sealand would now be automatically British), the outraged Bateses responded by declaring that they had also extended their territorial reach to twelve miles. This, they explained, meant the town of Felixstowe on the Suffolk coast now belonged to them.

Children

A naturalness. A lack of self-consciousness. The absence of the desire to judge. The ability to exist in the present, as if the past hadn't happened and the future were nothing to fear. A readiness to laugh and to forgive. A lack of side. A disinclination to cliquishness. Near freedom from sexuality. An experimental approach to food and drink. The willingness to try anything. Lack of interest in hygiene.

Lightness of touch. Delight in simplicity. An instinct for play. Imagination. Trust.

Children have just got it. No one taught them. They aren't putting it on. I don't know how long it lasts. Maybe in some cases, you lose it the first time you're attracted to a member of the opposite sex. Or it might happen when you engage in competitive sports, the first time you want to win. At the age of four or five, or a little later. But it's clear some people keep it a lot longer, and there are a few who never let it go. This childlike quality is one of the distinctive features of genius, prominent in its clearest instances in cultural history, such as Wolfgang Amadeus Mozart, Pablo Picasso and Albert Einstein. 'I do not know what I may appear to the world,' Isaac Newton once remarked, 'but to myself I seem to have been only like a boy playing on the sea shore, and diverting myself in now and then finding a smoother pebble or a prettier shell than ordinary.'

From the eternal student Hamlet* to the school-age heroes played by James Dean*, coolness has found its foremost expression in adolescent types. That has been *the* age, when the freedoms and physical strength of adulthood meet the spontaneity of childhood. Yet the childishness is key. It can be seen to link not only geniuses, but also many of those who defined and refined an idea of what cool means in the 20th century. Dean, definitely. But also Marlon Brando* and Paul Newman*. Bob Dylan*. Vivienne Westwood*. Richard Branson*. Madonna*. Björk*. In all these cases, it isn't hard to see the five-year-old concealed within the actor, singer, fashionista and entrepreneur.

Conchita Cintrón

History's most famous female bullfighter, Conchita Cintrón was always terrified before a performance. Once she was in the arena, however, her fear used to melt away. This was fortunate, she remarked, since 'A qualm or a cringe before 1,200 pounds of enraged bull is sure death.'

Brought up in Peru, the daughter of American parents, she became fascinated by the sport after taking riding lessons from a former bullfighter. She fought her first bull at fifteen. By eighteen, she was internationally renowned. Known as La Diosa de Oro (The Golden Goddess) on account of her mane of flowing blond hair, she drew attention as a young, attractive woman operating in a field dominated by men. She earned particular respect for her mastery of two styles of bullfighting: that of the Portuguese *rejoneador*, who faces the bull on horseback (and so is less likely to be gored), and that of the Spanish *toreador*, who performs on foot. While performing as a toreador, she was once so badly wounded that she was stretchered off to hospital. But she refused surgery and instead insisted on returning to the arena to kill her bull. This done, she promptly fainted.

It always riled Cintrón that, in Spain, women were forbidden to fight on foot, the supposed justification being that if one were gored, the more intimate parts of her body might have to be revealed by medics in the arena before the prurient eyes of thousands of spectators. In 1950, she was due to deliver what was billed as her last-ever performance, in the town of Jaén in southern Spain. Although down to fight as a rejoneador, she rode up to the official box and asked permission to fight as a toreador. This was refused. With a rush of blood to the head (she later said, 'I could not help myself') The Golden Goddess slipped off her horse and grabbed the cape and sword from the startled *novillero* (novice) who had been waiting to make the kill. She prepared the bull with a couple of passes; then, as it charged towards her, she dropped the sword, and instead of killing the beast, lovingly caressed it between the shoulders with the tips of her fingers (thereby also showing that she could have killed it). The crowd went wild. Hats and carnations were thrown at Cintrón's feet. She wept as she left the arena, and was immediately arrested. But the public protested so violently that the local governor released her, fearing a riot.

My wife

Writing this section, I toyed with the idea of including – perhaps concluding with – an entry on 'love'. But then it occurred to me that if I wrote one about my wife, that would amount to the same thing. I sometimes wonder why a preternaturally beautiful, free-thinking Russian, who skipped St Petersburg in her twenties during the chaotic period after the fall of Communism, would want to hang out with someone like me. And sometimes it seems she wonders too. While I tend to tie myself in verbal knots of evasion and euphemism, Anya is often very direct. I remember once asking her, during a conversation about

Socrates*, if she could ever love a man who was hideous. 'I think *you* are hideous,' she remarked. She later claimed that she thought the word 'hideous' meant 'eccentric', although I've always subsequently wondered if this was a retrospective improvisation.

Admittedly, there have been other occasional malapropisms that suggest her explanation may have been honest. She once told me that she had no respect for foreigners who came to England and refused to 'disintegrate'. She refers to hip hop singers as 'rappists', and on another occasion endearingly misremembered the title of the romantic comedy in which Bill Murray's misanthropic weatherman is forced to live the same day over and over again. She called it *The Day of the Badger*, which you could argue is actually a better title than *Groundhog Day*, although it might be more suited to a sci-fi horror film in which farmers finally get what's coming to them.

Many years ago, when I was single, a friend warned me that before he got married he was the most important person in his life. Afterwards, with a wife and child, he found himself demoted to number three. What he didn't say was that this painful process, which seems to be central to the enterprise of love, might have the desirable side-effect of making you cooler. I'm still resisting the process, but I can recognise the benefits of having one's self-love chipped away at: a sculptural task at which Anya exhibits the skill of a Rodin. I treasure the memory of the time I asked her what kind of men she goes for. 'Clowns,' she replied.

Lao Tzu

Be cool. That, in a nutshell, is the philosophy of the Ancient Chinese philosopher Lao Tzu as summarised in his book the *Tao Te Ching*, though there's a bit more to it than that. The Tao or 'Way' is a benign force that governs the universe, and the key to happiness is to live in accordance with it. In practice, this involves a combination of quietness, kindness, humility, humanity, not caring what other people think (whether good or ill), and making no distinction between success and failure. All of which prompts the response: nice work if you can get it.

Yet it has to be said that you're much more likely to get it if you take the trouble to read the book (preferably in the translation by Stephen Mitchell), which is a remarkable blend of poetry and practical advice. Its most intriguing concept is that of *wei wu wei*, literally 'doing not doing'. It's such a vague phrase that it's open to a wide range of interpretations. At its least controversial, it refers to a method for carrying out a task with such focus you cease to notice the effort involved or the time passing. When you finish, the result seems to have been effortless and immediate. Most of us have had this experience. The goal of the Tao master, however, is to make it his or her default gear, from when they wake up in the morning to when they go to bed at night.

Like Homer*, Lao Tzu may never have existed. His book may be the work of several authors. Yet the stories that have come down to us about his life are instructive. He's said to have been an archive keeper in one of the petty kingdoms of 6th-century BC China, and to have passed his life quietly until, in old age, he decided to set out on a water buffalo (a suitably lowly, slow-moving mode of transport) to cross the vast expanses of the country, before heading west into lands unknown. When he duly reached the border, the customs officer, on learning who he was, asked him first to write down his wisdom so it wouldn't be lost. This was a bold request. One of Lao Tzu's best-known maxims was the classic conversation-stopper, 'Those who know don't talk. Those who talk don't know.' We can only be grateful that he chose to make an exception on this occasion. Having handed over the first-ever copy of the *Tao Te Ching*, Lao Tzu wandered off and spent his remaining years impressing anyone who met him with how incredibly relaxed he was. The Buddha, some say, became his pupil.

Anti-celebrities

A story is told in Plato's *Republic* of how, after his death, the Greek hero Odysseus was asked in the Underworld what kind of person he would like to be in the next life. A great warrior perhaps? Or a powerful king? Neither, replied the man who had been both. He wanted to be a no one: a person of no consequence. (The Greek word is *apragmon*, meaning 'free from business'.) Odysseus, then, is perhaps the patron saint of 'anti-celebrities': people who possess enormous talents but have little desire for the fuss or hassle of the fame that would ensue if they allowed it to.

A nanny named Vivian Maier was found after her death

to have taken thousands of photographs, which in many cases she hadn't bothered to develop. The images have since earned her acclaim as one of the most gifted photographers of the 20th century. The novels of Elena Ferrante are adored by critics and public alike. Yet no one, apart from her publisher, knows who she is. The American singer-songwriter Sixto Rodriguez became a huge star in South Africa without even realising. On being informed of the fact many years later, his reaction was supremely relaxed.

A low-key contender for the title of the coolest man of all time, the singer-songwriter J.J. Cale merits a paragraph to himself. Never much of a megastar, in his day he was revered by the likes of Johnny Cash and Eric Clapton. (The latter called him his 'all-time favourite person'.) Cale's 'anti-Rubicon moment' – the point at which he might have become massive, but decided to step back – came in the 1970s when he was invited to perform his drowsy, bluesy single 'Crazy Mama' on a TV show watched by millions. He declined on hearing he would be expected to lip-sync, and the song reached only No. 22 in the charts, his biggest hit. Glance at the artwork of his albums and you notice something strange: he's not there. 'I always wanted to be a part of the show,' Cale once confessed. 'I never wanted to be the show.' As a motto, it sums up the anti-celebrity creed.

Tycho Brahe

If you were to invent a historical figure as an embodiment of cool, you might come up with someone a bit like the 16th-century scientist Tycho Brahe. Born into one of the richest families in Denmark, he was kidnapped by his uncle at the age of two, who brought him up as his own. At twenty, he lost part of his nose in a duel with his third cousin Manderup Parsberg, after they had argued about the validity of a mathematical formula. Brahe replaced the missing cartilage with a piece of brass, which he kept attached with a tube of glue that he carried with him everywhere. Some say he also had gold and silver nose-pieces to wear on more formal occasions.

His uncle died of pneumonia after saving the Danish king, Frederick II, from drowning. The inheritance made Tycho fabulously wealthy. To add to his fortunes, Frederick gifted him the island of Hven, where he built an observatory in which to pursue his lifelong passion for star-gazing. The scientist went on to build up the largest-ever collection of astronomical data, which he used to disprove Aristotle's assumption about the immutability of the heavens. In 1573 he published *De Nova Stella*, showing that, contrary to Aristotle's teaching, new stars are born. He went on to work on his magnum opus, the *Astronomiae Instauratae Progymnasmata* (Prelude to a New Astronomy). His obsessive records have led some to see him as a pioneer of the scientific revolution and a forerunner of the empiricists, although in truth Brahe was enough of a man of his time to be susceptible to the lure of less purely rational pursuits such as alchemy and astrology.

After Frederick died, he was succeeded by his son Christian, who was less of a Brahe fan. The latter was ousted from Hven and instead took up a post in Prague as astronomer to the Bohemian king and Holy Roman Emperor Rudolph II. In his downtime he enjoyed hanging out with a dwarf named Jepp, who used to sit under his table at mealtimes. He also had a pet elk with whom it's said he liked to engage in drinking contests. The unfortunate beast eventually died after drinking too much beer and falling down a flight of stairs. Brahe himself also seems to have perished in a drinking-related incident. During a banquet in Prague, he refused to go to the loo because he thought it was bad form and later perished of a ruptured bladder. Some, though, don't buy this story. They say he was poisoned, either by his pupil Johannes Kepler who wanted to get his hands on Brahe's data, or else at the behest of King Christian who believed Brahe had had an affair with his mother. This rumour of royal Danish adultery may conceivably have inspired Shakespeare when he came to write *Hamlet**.

Hypnagogia & hypnopompia

Forget drugs. There's a way of experiencing hallucinations that is legal, non-lethal and non-addictive. When you're feeling sleepy, sit in a chair and close your eyes. Let your head loll. And concentrate on what you can see behind your closed lids. At first it'll be the specks or circles of light called 'phosphenes'. But as you nod off, you'll enter an intermediary state called *hypnagogia* (from the Greek words for 'sleep' and 'leading to') which is accompanied by dream-like visions and also auditory hallucinations. You hear sounds and sentences. Something similar happens as you wake from sleep: a state called *hypnopompia*. And both conditions (the Italians have the same word for each) produce experiences that have inspired musicians, artists and authors.

Paul McCartney claims to have composed 'Yesterday' while in a hypnopompic state. Only the tune. At first, the words he put to it were not 'Yesterday' but 'Scrambled eggs', perhaps because this was what he was looking forward to having for his breakfast. Two of the most enduring horror stories of all time were created courtesy of hypnagogia. That was how Mary Shelley caught sight of the vision that led her to write *Frankenstein*. And Robert Louis Stevenson systematically relied on hypnagogia as a way to come up with ideas for his fiction. His technique was to lie flat on his back and raise both his arms vertically in the air. When he fell asleep, his arms would drop, and he used to wake up and remember the visions he had had. This was the genesis of the story that he would eventually publish as *The Strange Case of Dr Jekyll and Mr Hyde*.

Beethoven and Dalí also credit these phenomena with assisting their creativity. Scientists too. Isaac Newton, for one; for another, Dimitri Mendeleyev is said to have visualised how to arrange his Periodic Table of elements while drifting off to sleep in his chair one afternoon. There's a theory that hypnagogia and hypnopompia produce visual equivalents for one's deepest emotions and thoughts. This process, known as autosymbolism, was hypothesised by the somnologist

Herbert Silberer. Be warned, though. The approach can also produce more dubious results. One budding poet, who embraced hypnagogia as an aid to composition, came up with, 'Only God and Henry Ford / Have no umbilical cord.' It's not a couplet that is often anthologised.

The War Against Cliché by Martin Amis

I should have liked to have nominated Martin Amis's prose style, but there are good Amis books and bad Amis books. The conventional wisdom (which in this instance, contrary to convention, is probably wise) is that the British author's fiction peaked with the 1984 novel *Money* and has since been on a downward trend. This, though, brings to mind the smart response of Joseph Heller to the interviewer who took him to task for never having subsequently written another novel as good as *Catch-22*. 'Who has?' he demanded. Who *has* published anything as cool, funny and stylistically slick as *Money* since 1984? One answer, if you allow non-fiction writing, is Amis himself, in the form of his 2001 collection of literary journalism, *The War Against Cliché*.

If you want to see William S. Burroughs* berated, Norman Mailer* nailed to the page and Andy Warhol* well and truly slated, this is the book to reach for. Warhol's voluminously vapid diaries, Amis notes, contain not a single interesting insight about art. The 'essentially humourless' Mailer writes to pay his alimony bills. Burroughs' 1971 novel *The Wild Boys*, meanwhile, is dismissed as 'of only academic interest to the heterosexual reader'. The best phrase to characterise Amis the literary critic is 'phrase-maker'. In his foreword, he wryly describes his self-consciously flamboyant twenty-something self, with his 'shoulder-length hair, a flower shirt and knee-high boots (well-concealed, it is true, by the twin tepees of my flared trousers)'. In prose, too, his has always been a dandy-ish style, like that of Tom Stoppard, say, or Kenneth Tynan: infectious but inimitable.

It's rebellious to be good, because most people aren't. To be this good seems almost revolutionary. And although there's plenty here on his heroes, with whole sections devoted to the virtues of Philip Larkin and Vladimir Nabokov, Amis is never better than when using his words as weapons. That's his metaphor, in a rare moment (in this book) of self-importance, when he comes to review the Thomas Harris thriller *Hannibal*, which other critics had hailed as a master-piece. 'My pen flashes from its scabbard', he tells us, rather portentously. But what follows does justice to the claim. Harris's fat novel is turned to ticker tape. *The War Against Cliché* is a joy. A lesson.

The history of the heart shape

The heart shape shouldn't really be called the heart shape, since it's not the shape of a heart. If you were performing heart surgery, you'd be taken aback if you opened someone's chest and found an organ with a perfectly rounded, indented top and smoothly pointed bottom. An actual heart looks more like an over-ripe potato, with an aorta sprouting from the top like a new shoot. Or it might be compared to 'a fist wrapped in blood', to use a phrase of the playwright Patrick Marber.

Strictly speaking, the 'heart shape' isn't cool. Stamped on countless fatuous Valentine's cards, it has become the emblem for a simplistic modern concept of love, which is arguably responsible for the unhappiness of millions. But the *history* of the heart shape, and how it came to be associated with the organ we have for some reason chosen to view as the seat of the emotions, is far grittier and edgier than you might think. Seedier, too, quite literally. As a shape, it was stamped on coins issued in the north African town of Cyrene in the 7th century BC, where it indicated the shape of the seedpod of a herb named silphium, which was in high demand as a menagogue. In other words, silphium was said to bring on menstruation and could therefore be used as a contraceptive. The demand was so great that the herb was harvested to extinction. But by then a connection had been forged: between sex and the shape of the silphium seedpod.

From there, it was a shorter step to link that shape to the heart, once the heart became associated with love. It was emblazoned on playing cards, adopted by Christian iconographers, and later commandeered by Victorian sentimentalists who were inventing love with a capital L around the same time as they were coming up with the idea of Santa Claus. If this all sounds a bit unromantic, maybe so (although not nearly as unromantic as an alternative theory, which suggests the heart shape was actually inspired by the twin curves of a woman's breasts or buttocks, or possibly her pubic mound, or vulva). In any case, seeing the heart shape for what it is just clears the way for real, realistic love. And that's what real romance is all about.

Jack Johnson

In the early decades of professional boxing, white heavyweight boxing champions refused to fight black challengers. It was beneath them, they said. But an additional reason was Jack Johnson. A massive, shaven-headed black boxer known as the Galveston Giant, he was an oddly genial presence in the ring, always smiling, and tending to hang back, waiting for his opponent to tire. He would even help to prop him up, if he looked likely to fall, to prolong the fight for the entertainment of spectators. Having won the World Colored Heavyweight Championship in 1903, he got a crack at the full Heavyweight title only in 1908, after spending two years literally pursuing the champion, Tommy Burns, around the world, taunting him at every opportunity.

In the event, Johnson destroyed him. He was so in control of the contest, he goaded him with mocking jibes (albeit milder than the racist onslaught Burns had launched against him in Round 1). 'Who told you you were a fighter, Tommy?' Johnson asked. 'You hit like a girl.' Or, 'Hit me here,' he suggested, pointing at some part of his body, while Burns, exhausted, flailed. This was what angered those who were already outraged at the thought of a black champion: his insouciant cockiness. Away from the ring, he dressed in finely tailored suits and dandyish hats. His teeth were capped with gold. He listened to opera, played the fiddle, and read voraciously in three languages (particularly favouring the novels of Alexandre Dumas). Most controversially of all, he had a penchant for white girlfriends, which he flaunted. 'I have the right to choose who my mate shall be without the dictation of any man,' he once declared. 'I am not a slave.'

Sceptics said Burns had never been much of a champion. The real master was Jim Jeffries, they claimed, a white former World Heavyweight title holder who had never lost a fight. He was coaxed reluctantly out of retirement in 1910 to face the Galveston Giant in what was billed as 'the battle of the century'. The political implications were huge. As Johnson entered the ring, the mainly white crowd chanted, 'Kill the nigger!' while the band struck up the popular tune 'All Coons Look Alike to Me'. Johnson destroyed Jeffries too. Muhammad Ali* would later be inspired by the example of the former's personal style, his obduracy in the face of widespread loathing, and his courage. 'He faced the world unafraid,' Johnson's third wife Irene observed at his funeral. 'There wasn't anybody or anything he feared.'

La Belle Noiseuse

There's nothing written in stone that says a film has to be around two hours long. It's just that that's about the length of time most people can go before they need to pay a visit to the lavatory. That and the fact that, since this is what we've grown accustomed to, anything over a couple of hours is going to feel on the long side. *La Belle Noiseuse* (1991) by the French New Wave auteur Jacques Rivette is nearly four hours in length. But curb your fear. The canny director soothes our attention by the cunning device of having Emmanuelle Béart, who was then arguably the most beautiful woman in the world, appear stark naked in almost every scene.

The film has nothing to do with sex, or not directly, at least. Béart, as the irritable, irresistible Marianne, reluctantly agrees to pose for a reclusive artistic genius named Frenhofer (Michel Piccoli), who has barely painted anything in years. He hopes that her beauty may inspire him to complete a potential masterpiece he once abandoned, an epic canvas entitled 'La Belle Noiseuse' (The Beautiful Troublemaker), which first time round he attempted with his wife Liz (Jane Birkin) as his model. Much of the film consists of Frenhofer staring at the naked Marianne with abstracted focus, and Marianne glaring away angrily. Caveat: anyone who doesn't want the story ruined should now skip to the last paragraph, as the next one contains a substantial spoiler.

When Liz views the finished painting (which we never get to see) she is devastated by the realisation that Marianne has inspired the fire in Frenhofer that she never quite could. The artist, who up until this point has seemed entirely egotistical, regrets the pain this causes her. Without telling anyone, he places 'La Belle Noiseuse' in an alcove of his studio, and bricks it up. When his dealer, Porbus, comes to inspect the work, he palms him off with some commonplace substitute that he quickly knocks up. The point is that what's important for Frenhofer is to have taken his talent to its extreme conclusion. His genius has found its form. Whether or not this is revealed to the wider public is immaterial to him.

The film is based on a short story by Honoré de Balzac called *The Unknown Masterpiece*. The Balzac version was so beloved of the painter Cézanne that he once declared, 'Frenhofer, c'est moi!' Picasso was also a fan. In tribute, he moved to Paris's rue des Grands-Augustins, where part of the story takes place, and it was here that he painted his own masterpiece, 'Guernica'.

142½ Fulham Road

For a range of reasons, I have very rarely been on a date. Yet to my surprise I found myself going on one late in 1998. I arranged to meet the girl in question at a pub beside the Thames near where I had been doing an internship at a bank. It had been a difficult week. My mentor at the company, which specialised in bonds, had kept introducing me with the words, 'This is Thomas. He doesn't know a bond from a secret agent.' It was a fair criticism, but not one that was designed to put me at my ease. On the plus side, it meant that when I went along for this date, I was wearing a suit.

Things got off to a good start. After a drink, I showed the girl, whose name was Alison, a poem I'd written when

I should have been studying bonds, and she seemed to like it. We had a couple more drinks, then agreed to go for dinner. At the time the only decent restaurant I knew was in Chelsea. We crossed the city to reach it. As we walked along the Fulham Road, it began raining so hard that we were getting wet despite my umbrella. Alison spotted the entrance to an expensive-looking restaurant, and because it was raining, and I was slightly drunk, we stepped inside. A man took my umbrella and our coats. He then handed each of us a glass of champagne. That was when we realised that this was not a restaurant at all but someone's home, where a private party was taking place. I suppose the reason we weren't challenged was that I was suitably dressed, and Alison always looked terrific. We glanced at each other. 'I'm up for it if you are,' she said. Not wanting to seem lame, I nodded. But I suggested we mingled separately for half an hour as that way we were less likely to get busted.

It was a very flash party, a celebration of someone's fortieth birthday. The guests were glamorous, international types. The waitresses were wearing sexy Santa Claus outfits. (Can I be remembering this right?) I was surprised by how easy it was to pass undetected. You just let people finish your sentences. 'So how long have you known …?' I asked, and the person I was talking to supplied the name of the birthday boy. Occasionally I would catch the eye of Alison across the room. Then we joined forces and had fun chatting with strangers. We left after an hour or two, not wanting to push our luck. I later realised that the entrance door was one I had often noticed before, because it was the only door in a long red-brick wall and it had always previously been closed. The street number was 142½. I've never seen it open since. Alison and I went out together for a while after that. I think she lives in India now.

Solitude

If solitude were a species, it would be listed as endangered. Most of us these days carry our mobile phones around with us. We're never too far from a wifi signal that would enable us to check our email or log on to Facebook and see what our friends are up to. If you listen, you can usually hear sounds of human life, laughter in the next room, or the revving of an engine. So it's tempting to conclude that we're somehow afraid of solitude, as if it constituted a kind of failure, the opposite of love. As if solitude automatically entailed a feeling of loneliness. As if it offered no allure.

Yet three of the world's major religions – Islam, Christianity* and Buddhism* – were created after a period of solitude on the part of their founders. And many great authors have sought out or endured their equivalent of forty days in the wilderness, and found inspiration there. The psychologist Carl Jung used to hunker down in the ascetic Bollingen Tower on the shore of Lake Zurich, which he had built himself. Ludwig Wittgenstein emerged from periods spent alone in a hut in Norway declaring that he had solved *all* philosophical problems, as in a sense he had. Even

enforced solitude can have its consolations. It was while serving a jail term in Bedfordshire for religious malpractice that
John Bunyan began the book that would become *The Pilgrim's
Progress*. Cervantes said he had the idea for Don Quixote in
prison: a remark usually thought to refer to some months he
spent incarcerated in Seville for debt, although the citizens of
Ulcinj claim he may have sketched out the plot while locked
up in their town on the coast of Montenegro, having been
taken prisoner at the battle of Lepanto.

Reading is a form of solitude. As is meditation or going
for a walk. As, often, is a journey. And when you remember
the mood of peace those activities can bring, as the mind
gives an order to thoughts that had been chaotic, it seems
strange that longer periods of chosen solitude should be
so countercultural. Sigmund Freud is partly to blame, for
the emphasis he put on requited love as the ultimate sign of
psychological well-being. It's often supposed that those who
spend time alone do so because they're ill at ease in company.
But in fact it's as often true that those who are most at ease in
company are most likely to be comfortable alone. So perhaps
if you acquire the capacity for solitude you'll be more worthy
of company.

Socrates

In Athens in the 5th century BC, a fat, bald, extremely ugly
man wandered around barefoot interviewing self-important
people such as philosophers and politicians. He confessed

to knowing nothing about anything, and insisted that he merely wished to learn. Yet the strange thing was, as the chat proceeded, it became clear the interviewee was the ignorant one, while the fat man actually seemed pretty clued up. This was Socrates, employing his 'dialectical method' of question-and-answer, which is one of the cornerstones of western philosophy.

The problem with Socrates is he never bothered to write anything down, so our only idea of him comes from accounts by others. Primarily his pupil Plato, who presents him as a total legend. A brave soldier as well as a bumptious inter-viewer, Socrates served in the Peloponnesian War, and stood his ground when all around him turned and fled. He could drink anyone under the table. And despite his appearance, he was so clever everyone fancied him. Yet being Socrates, he wasn't especially interested in sex. Ugly men through the ages have used their brains to try to charm people into bed. Socrates seems to have gone to bed with people mainly so he could talk to them about philosophy. But this, as we've noted, was according to Plato, who had a strange belief in 'ideal forms'. There was an ideal form of a chair, he said, and of beauty, and everything else. Socrates, perhaps, was his ideal form of a philosopher.

Yet even if the Socrates we know is a fictional creation, he's an incredibly inspiring one. He was eventually put on trial for 'corrupting the youth' (in that he encouraged them to question their elders) and 'not believing in the city's gods' such as Zeus and Athena and the rest (which seems reasonable in retrospect). One thing he did believe in was democracy. Since he was found guilty of the charges, he submitted to his death sentence, despite having the opportunity to escape. With his friends around him in his prison cell, all weeping and tearing their hair, he calmly drank the poison he was given. His last words were: 'We owe a cock to Asclepius' (meaning perhaps that death would come to him as a cure and consequently they should make an offering to the god of healing). So did he, after all, believe in the city's gods? With Socrates, right to the end, it wasn't easy to be sure what he really thought.

Victoria

A girl dances in a Berlin nightclub. She is Spanish, 20-something, and sufficiently pretty (her smile makes you want to smile) to light up her seedy surroundings. She's having a good time or trying to. Alone, a little lonely, she attempts to chat up the hipster barman but he's not interested. Then, as she's leaving, because she has to go to work the next day, she falls in with a group of likeable Berliner low-lifes, led by the courteous Sonne. These are the opening few minutes of *Victoria* (2015), whose plot eventually sees the eponymous heroine being roped into an armed robbery, with devastating consequences.

The narrative is Dickensian. It's like an extended version of that scene in *Oliver Twist* when the naive hero, on the loose in London, realises that his new friends are doing more than playing games. And put like that, the movie may not sound so remarkable. But when you learn that it was filmed in one unbroken shot – the cameraman doggedly following the actors around Berlin for the entirety of its 148-minute running time – you may be more inclined to believe there is something special here. The 'one shot' film has recently become trendy, promising an aura of truth in an era of CGI trickery, yet in the case of *Victoria* it's more than a gimmick. It's appropriate to the tale being told, of a girl who finds herself on a ride she can't get off, the vertiginous fear growing until it becomes almost unbearable. And it also seems fitting that her character's risk-taking was mirrored by the director, Sebastian Schipper, and his crew and cast. According to Schipper, he could only afford to try the experiment three times. The first two were duds. 'There is no plan B,' he told his actors before their third attempt. 'Give them your heart,' he urged. 'Feel it. Be afraid.' The pep talk seems to have worked.

Victoria is a story of romance and violence, but one of the things that makes it so effective is that neither of those elements is explicit. The romance is restrained, limited to the sight of two characters who above all seem to like each other. The violence too is understated, suggested rather than shown. For all the air of improvisation (the script the actors started with was just a few pages long), there's a canny hand at work. The finished film barely lasts more than two hours but it seems to accommodate a lifetime. It does something that blockbusters rarely manage, presenting you with characters you care about and will miss. Its contained concentration and concision make it gemlike in a way that long-form TV drama, for all its virtues, can never be. It does things that only a film can.

Mark Rylance

It's tempting to be dismissive of actors as vain, flimsy creatures, whose skill is to seem more interesting than they are. So let's swerve the other way, just for a moment. The very greatest performers, the ones who vanish into a role, the chameleons who can play villains, heroes, jocks and nerds, do more than merely dazzle with their talent. They embody the possibility of change. A great actor demonstrates repeatedly an empowering fluidity of personality: if they can be anyone, the message is, then maybe anyone can. This grandiose kind of claim cannot be made for many, but the British actor Mark Rylance seems to justify it.

His Johnny Rooster Byron in Jez Butterworth's play *Jerusalem* was a rip-roaring roister-doister. As Thomas Cromwell in TV's *Wolf Hall*, he was watchful, each scene's silent centre of gravity. Playing Richard III at London's Globe Theatre, he was almost an idiot. The result was terrifying, the sadism apparently a revenge on nature for his disability. What these three had in common was they were all outsiders who wrote their own rules: a quality they shared with their creator. As a child, Rylance suffered from a speech impediment that meant no one could understand him. He found it easier to communicate when acting, and always tried to hang on to that childlike quality of play in his adult performances. Sometimes his opinions can seem childlike, too. He's fascinated by the dubious mysteries of crop circles and ley lines, and suspects that Shakespeare may not have written the plays attributed to him. Yet the actor's quiet air of intelligence is such, one questions one's own assumptions. Maybe there *is* some kind of special energy at the Rollright Stones in Oxfordshire. Maybe one *should* go there and see for oneself.

For years, Rylance was a wonderful kind of anti-celebrity*: the greatest actor most people had never heard of. His anti-Rubicon moment (when he could have become a star but took a step back) came in the 1980s when Steven Spielberg offered him a role in *Empire of the Sun*. Rylance declined in order to do a season of Shakespeare. Maybe he regretted that decision at times, but as he likes to point out, it led almost immediately to his meeting his wife, the composer Claire Van Kampen, so it 'turned out to be an alright call'. Three decades later, Spielberg reached out to him again, and their collaboration in the film *Bridge of Spies* led to the actor's first Oscar and a new level of recognition. We just have to hope he doesn't stop performing on stage, now he's famous. I saw his Richard III. It wasn't that he was better than the other actors. It was as if they were acting well, but he was doing something different. I wouldn't even call it acting. The director Tim Carroll put it well when he said of Rylance, 'he seems to have more time than anyone else'.

Lila Says by Anonymous

In 1996, an anonymous French novella called *Lila Says* became an international bestseller. In brief, it's the story of a shy immigrant, Chimo, whose life on a Paris sink estate is transformed by a blonde teenager named Lila who likes to talk dirty to him. She tells him all the filthy things she's got up to recently, though it's never clear if she's telling the truth or just making it up to excite him. Understandably dazzled into inaction, he obsesses about Lila until his sexist mates get together and gang-rape her. That's about it, as far as the plot's concerned. And whether or not you're impressed will depend on your attitude to pornography and, perhaps, on how old you are. When I read it in English translation in 1997, it struck me as a masterpiece.

Looking back, I think the coolest thing about it is the story of how it came to be written. According to the 'French Publisher's Note' in my enthusiastically-thumbed edition, the manuscript reached them via a lawyer, in the form of two exercise books delivered by hand. Inside, the novel was scrawled in almost indecipherable biro. The idea was that it was the work of an inspired illiterate. It came straight, that is to say, from the foul rag and bone shop of the heart. But was it true, this sales pitch? I'm not sure it matters, since it wins out either way on the cool front.

If it's true, case closed. But even if it's a hoax, it's one that's pulled off with an impressive degree of chutzpah. Rereading it recently, I must admit, I was fairly sure it was a hoax. There are bits, it seems to me, that couldn't have been written by someone who, as the narrator claims, never 'read a book right through'. It's not that these passages are bad. It's that they're generic, which is to say they're written by someone who has read a lot. Yet let's not forget that *Lila Says* impressed the novelist Fay Weldon, who, although she too was convinced it was a hoax, lavished it with praise. As did the popular philosopher Alain de Botton, who called it 'essential reading', 'beautifully written', and (in a moment of passion) 'very sexy'.

I like the fact that, whoever wrote it – whether it was one author or, as Weldon suspected, several – they had the self-restraint not to reveal themselves even after the book became a hit. I like the fact that it's a fiction about fiction, with a claim to truth that raises questions about the respective merits of truth and fiction. And I love the fact that the supermodel Kate Moss* named her daughter Lila, born in 2002, after the book's sex-fantasy heroine.

A tobacconist in Corfu Town

I don't know whether or not smoking is cool, but I'll tell you what isn't cool: the smoking ban. Which is why I'd say one of the coolest traits that has been displayed by the Greek nation over this past disastrous decade (as one after another of its governments has flailed and folded) has been its insouciant refusal to abide by this least appealing of laws. Visit Athens now, or wander the bars and cafés of Nafplio or Nafpaktos (Lepanto as once was), and you'll see that everyone is still at it. There are *kafeneia* (the caffeinated equivalent of local pubs) in hill villages where the very idea of stopping anyone smoking is a joke. Ashtrays stand their ground on every tabletop, whether indoors or out, in defiance of the latest lawmakers.

There was a time when it looked as if it might go the other way. Following the ban of 2009, which was refined in 2011, it was reported that the minister of health had appointed 800 'smoke police' to enforce the new ruling. Then we heard that the prime minister George Papandreou had been given a World No Tobacco Day award (catchy title?) for his 'political courage' in passing a smoking ban in a country where social smoking had become such an integral part of the culture. Six months later, Papandreou was out of a job. Since then, although a few of the top hotels have become no-smoke zones, the prohibition has been widely flouted, with people continuing to smoke when and where they please. Latest reports suggest that 42 per cent of Greeks are smokers, the highest percentage of any EU country. In 2013, a group of MPs complained that their colleagues were puffing away *inside the parliament building.*

In Corfu Town, where I like to spend as much time as possible, there's a tobacconist that may be the most beautiful shop in the world. It occupies the sharp end of a V where two side-streets converge on Nikiforos Theotokis street and it's only big enough for two or three customers at a time. It seems to be built out of cigarettes. A sign above the door proclaims 'Nikos Agathos, 1941, Tobacco House'. The ancient owner, Nikos, has worked there for 75 years straight, with the exception of 27 months when he served in the army. He and his wife Irene seem to make up their hours as they go along. The place is often locked. It has a magical air, as though, if you're lucky enough to find it open, it might transport you back in time.

'For Emma, Forever Ago' by Bon Iver

Late in 2006, a sensitive, bearded 25-year-old singer-songwriter named Justin Vernon was plunged into depression by the break-up of his band and the end of a relationship. He drove through the night from California to his home state of Wisconsin and holed up for the winter in a log cabin belonging to his father. During the three months he spent there, he hunted his own food, shooting a couple of deer, whose meat lasted for his stay, he said later, 'and then some'. One night, a bear blundered into the cabin, smelling his stew, but he chased it away.

Although he'd brought his guitar, Vernon hadn't planned on writing any music while he was there. But he happened to have some recording equipment with him, and when his mood of introspection, concentrated by solitude, triggered memories of his break-up with his first love, Sara Emma Jensen, the songs began to come. At first they were just melodies. He employed an aleatory or random technique for coming up with the lyrics, improvising the right sounds, and then listening back to the recordings, and seeing what words they resembled. The result was a collection of nine songs whose lyrics are obscure to the point of incomprehensibility.

On one, he croons that the sky is 'the womb' and 'you are the moon', whatever that might mean. The chord progressions are simple. But by a chance alchemy, it works. *Rolling Stone* magazine has called 'For Emma, Forever Ago' 'one of the all-time great break-up albums'.

Almost the entire work – which is at once heartwarming and heartbreaking – is Vernon's, but he formed a band to tour the songs, and called it Bon Iver. He had spent some of his evenings in the cabin rewatching old episodes of the TV show *Northern Exposure*, in which 'Bon hiver' is used as a greeting: 'Good winter'. It was a fitting phrase, since it had been a good winter for Vernon. Enjoyably, he has revealed in an interview that, while some might have expected the experience to have been cathartic, he didn't feel 'renewed' by the creation of the album. He had arrived at the cabin suffering from a liver infection, and it was still troubling him when he left. So it's also one of the all-time great liver infection albums.

Heinrich 'Harry' Beck

I first met Harry at a party at 142½ Fulham Road*, which I gatecrashed accidentally after mistaking someone's private home for a restaurant. What I most remember about him that first evening was his slim pale face and slicked-back fair hair, his way of talking softly with a wry smile, as if language were a blunt tool for conveying his meaning, and a ring he wore that he told me was designed as a weapon. If anyone attacked him, he would swipe it across their forehead, causing a curtain of blood to descend, which would render them temporarily blind.

For a year we communicated only in song recommendations. His were obscure, confined to B-sides and remixes. (One that I remember was 'I Love My Man (The Lazyboy's Anyone For Tennis Remix)' by Bent.) Then we met up a few times in a pub by the Thames where the former footballer George Best, who was a friend of Harry's, used to prop up the bar. I was going through a bad time in my private life, and Harry listened. He had that Gatsby-esque trick of seeming to have a better impression of me than I deserved, which helped. I felt ashamed, meanwhile, at how little I learnt about him. It's his way. He is evasive, revealing himself only in fragments. He once mentioned that he has a passion for tulips, dating from a time he worked as a gardener on the island of Stromboli, because he was romantically obsessed with the woman who owned the next-door villa.

Variously gifted, but apparently unambitious, he once entered a poem under the pseudonym Karl-Christian von Lippert Weillersheim into the *Literary Review*'s poetry contest, after I told him I was one of the judges. He admitted to this only after being awarded the monthly prize: an achievement that seemed all the more impressive given that English isn't his first language, which is German, or even his second, which is French. He put both to use during a later stint as a chef in a Swiss ski resort, where he and I hung out while I worked on another of my unpublishable novels. It was during this period that his drinking got out of hand, as I learnt one evening when he head-butted me to the floor. When I asked how I had annoyed him, he replied, 'You've got issues.' He later claimed to have no memory of the incident. Life has been tough for Harry, more recently, I suspect. His weight has really ballooned. The last I heard, he was in California, engaged in a fourteen-year course of Taoist study.

'In the Summertime' by Mungo Jerry

The list of the bestselling singles of all time makes depressing reading. The top ten includes Elton John telling Princess Diana that she lived her life like a candle in the wind, and Celine Dion. But coming in at number four, with estimated total sales of 30 million, is an exception. 'In the Summertime', released in 1970, was the debut single of Mungo Jerry, a British band named after a villainous cat from a T.S. Eliot poem. One reason for its success was that it was the first 'maxi single', meaning the record had three songs on it rather than the usual two, which made it seem good value. Another was that it was about the spirit of the summer, with the result that DJs reliably reach for it every year, as soon as hot weather strikes.

But the song is more than just about the spirit of summer. It embodies it. A jaunty skiffle tune, meaning a jazz–blues–folk hybrid partly played on home-made instruments, it has the joyful air of being improvised on the spot, an impression that is backed up by lead singer Ray Dorset's claim that he wrote it in ten minutes. Dorset, who was from Middlesex, was something to look at, with his curly afro and massive sideburns, the cheeky grin revealing a startling gap between the front teeth, and an endearingly nervous look as he eyed the camera during an accompanying video, which was performed on the central reservation in front of the Hilton Hotel on Park Lane, with the traffic streaming past on either side.

The assorted noises heard on the song include the revving of a car's engine, the shaking of a cabasa, and one of the band members sporadically blowing raspberries into the neck of a large glass bottle. Meanwhile Dorset sings about the way in which, when the sun comes out, a young man's fancy lightly turns to thoughts of love (I'm paraphrasing). He'll try to pick someone up, have a couple of drinks and take her for a drive. This was back in the days when the combination of those activities was thought to be OK. The 24-year-old Dorset proceeds to explain the general philosophy of his generation, which is to 'love everybody' but do as he likes. He also says he's keen to spend time fishing or swimming in the sea.

Being uncool

It isn't cool to be too cool, just as it isn't charming to be too charming. If you're too charming, people suspect that they're being manipulated. If you're too cool, it doesn't seem real. You need the behavioural equivalent of a Persian flaw, the deliberate break in the pattern that Persian carpet-makers are said to weave into their designs because only God is entitled to create something perfect. Paradoxically, it's this that makes the carpet perfect. Beau Brummell's vanity. Marlene Dietrich's lisp. Humphrey Bogart's use of wigs. Tennessee Williams's moustache. Jesse Owens's self-promotion. Norman Mailer's shortness. Marlon Brando's obesity. Nina Simone's curious style of dancing. Bob Dylan's appearance in the film *Hearts of Fire*.

There's a kind of coolness in uncoolness. Why did Irvine Welsh choose the title *Trainspotting* for his 1993 novel about a group of Scottish drug addicts? OK, partly it was because when he was growing up in Edinburgh, 'trainspotting' was a euphemism for doing drugs, but that in itself, on one level, was because it was a proverbially uncool activity. To disparage the seedy glamour of heroin addiction as 'trainspotting' ensures cool status by dismissing it. The following year saw the release of the movie *Forrest Gump*, whose persistent message is that it's cooler to be uncool than to be cool. The hero's friends Lieutenant Dan, and Jenny, the love of his life, are both children of the counterculture, but it makes them miserable. Whereas Gump, the holy innocent, is a surprisingly effective human being. And if there's one thing he really doesn't care about, it's being cool.

I'm not suggesting now, at five to midnight, that coolness is a waste of time. It can, let's say, encourage a certain superficiality, a focus on style over substance, but it needn't. The habit of questioning authority, the compulsion to live creatively, the ability to control your emotions when necessary – these will always be desired and admired. It's only that, if you take it all too seriously, you can't achieve it. There has to be a part of you that doesn't care about cool, that's willing to be utterly uncool. Otherwise, you don't stand a chance.

Appendix: The Cool Test

How cool are you? Learn the truth by taking this swift multiple-choice quiz, which measures your cool rating according to the Nine Defining Qualities of Cool.

In each case, pick the statements that most accurately describe you or your beliefs. Then tot up your final score, using the scoring system provided at the end.

1. Style

a) You have a natural physical grace and an instinctive flair for clothes. It's not wholly absurd to think that you might one day start your own fashion line.

b) You favour the neutral look: aka the Everyman style. You feel that clothes are not that interesting and not that important. It's what's inside that counts.

c) Style may not be your strong suit. People assume your wardrobe choices are ironic. Occasionally, someone asks, 'Are you really planning to go out like that?'

2. Rebellion

a) To arms! The world has gone to hell. The rich are loathsome and the poor are powerless. The whole system stinks and what's needed is a revolution.

b) Rules are usually there for a reason. You avoid rocking the boat unless you have to. If something annoys you, you complain through the proper channels.

c) Nothing commands your automatic respect. You judge each case on its merits and decide whether to play ball or follow a course of quiet defiance.

3. Rootlessness

a) You own your own home or hope to. You may trade it in for a bigger home if finances allow. The ideal is a secure and spacious single place in which to raise a healthy family.

b) Wherever you lay your hat, that's your home. You get itchy feet if you stay in the same place for more than a few months. Movement is freedom.

c) Your work requires or allows regular travel. Each time you set out for the airport, you thrill to life's myriad possibilities. You're interested in foreign property prices.

4. Recklessness

a) Anyone who smokes is clearly an idiot. Not to mention irresponsible in terms of the burden they place on the health service. The occasional drink is all right.

b) You might be hit by a car tomorrow so you may as well enjoy life. Skiing? Definitely. Sky diving? Why not? Base jumping? Sounds interesting. It's all about the rush.

c) You like to drink – a lot, sometimes. You have the odd cheeky cigarette at parties. It kind of annoys you to be told to wear a seat belt in the back of a car.

5. Promiscuity/Celibacy

a) Love is the greatest thing that can happen to anyone. It leads naturally to a commitment that lasts, and with luck, is the foundation stone for building a family.

b) Love – in the sense of boy meets girl and both live happily ever after – was invented by Hollywood. You do what's right for you and don't care how you're judged.

c) Love means sex in your twenties and marriage in your thirties. You'd be furious if your partner cheated, but you might cheat, if fairly sure of not being found out.

6. Self-Expression

a) You work in one of the professions. You prefer non-fiction books to novels and would take a good blockbuster over some arthouse nonsense. You think poetry is boring.

b) You are an artist/musician/writer (basically you're a *creative* type) and good at what you do. Alternatively or in addition, you regard your life as a work of art.

c) You don't write novels but you love to read them. You dabble in photography. You feel you have a strong creative side but have never found the right outlet for it.

7. Flamboyance/Austerity

a) You're a natural showman – some would say a show-off. If you're gay, no one's in any doubt about it. If you're straight, some have suspected otherwise.

b) Solitude appeals. The simple life. A hut on a mountainside. A houseboat, perhaps. Sometimes pretty much everything most people care about seems ridiculous.

c) You acted a bit at school but suffer from a mild form of stage fright. Still, you can make a reasonable enough speech when you absolutely have to.

8. Taciturnity/Eloquence

a) Chatting on the phone isn't really your thing. That said, after a few drinks, it's sometimes hard to get you to shut up.

b) Words are your friends, the tools, perhaps, of your trade. Sometimes in conversation, you feel like a jazz musician improvising a solo.

c) 'They don't say much. But you know that when they do, they really mean it' – a comment you could imagine being made about you.

9. Emotional Self-Control

a) You cry a lot. Or if you're not a crier, you're prone to lose your temper. You don't see what's wrong with this. Emotions shouldn't be bottled up.

b) No one could call you a psychopath but you get annoyed when you're treated unfairly. You're more likely to cry in a movie than at a funeral.

c) If someone hit you, you'd just feel bad for them. You almost never lose your cool, and indeed rarely feel strongly about anything. You're basically super-chilled.

* * *

Scoring system:

1. a) 2   b) 1   c) 0
2. a) 1   b) 0   c) 2
3. a) 0   b) 2   c) 1
4. a) 0   b) 2   c) 1
5. a) 1   b) 2   c) 0
6. a) 0   b) 2   c) 1
7. a) 1   b) 2   c) 0
8. a) 0   b) 1   c) 2
9. a) 0   b) 1   c) 2

What your total score means:

0–6 Coolness clearly isn't a big priority for you. Or if it is, you should probably rethink your approach.

7–12 You're unlikely to found your own religion but you're reasonably cool. You have your moments.

13–18 When it comes to cool, you don't need any lessons. If anything, you should be giving the lessons.

Index

Also available

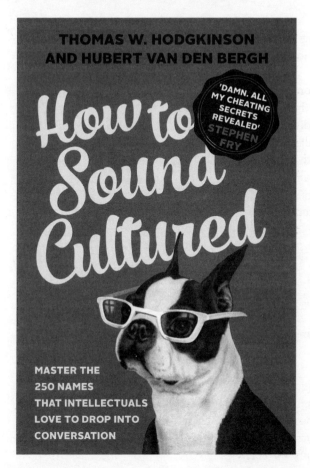

Which philosopher had the maddest hairstyle?
Which novelist drank 50 cups of black coffee every day?
What on earth did Simone de Beauvoir see in Jean-Paul Sartre?

Become an overnight culture vulture with this wry and yet
profoundly useful look inside the mirrored palaces of high culture.

'Damn. All my cheating secrets revealed. In book form.'
Stephen Fry

ISBN: 978-178578-093-6 (paperback)
ISBN: 978-184831-931-8 (ebook)